God's Quad

God's Quad

Small Faith Communities on Campus and Beyond

edited by

Kevin Ahern and
Christopher Derige Malano

ORBIS BOOKS
Maryknoll, New York 10545

Founded in 1970, Orbis Books endeavors to publish works that enlighten the mind, nourish the spirit, and challenge the conscience. The publishing arm of the Maryknoll Fathers and Brothers, Orbis seeks to explore the global dimensions of the Christian faith and mission, to invite dialogue with diverse cultures and religious traditions, and to serve the cause of reconciliation and peace. The books published reflect the views of their authors and do not represent the official position of the Maryknoll Society. To learn more about Maryknoll and Orbis Books, please visit our website at www.maryknollsociety.org.

Manufactured in the United States of America.
Manuscript editing and typesetting by Joan Weber Laflamme.

Library of Congress Cataloging-in-Publication Data

Names: Ahern, Kevin, editor.
Title: God's quad : small faith communities on campus and beyond / Kevin Ahern and Christopher Derige Malano, editors.
Description: Maryknoll : Orbis Books, 2018. | Includes bibliographical references and index.
Identifiers: LCCN 2018006179 (print) | LCCN 2018023495 (ebook) | ISBN 9781608337538 (ebook) | ISBN 9781626982871 (pbk.)
Subjects: LCSH: Catholic college students—Religious life. | Universities and colleges—Religion. | Church work with college students—Catholic Church. | Christian communities—Catholic Church.
Classification: LCC BX2347.8.S8 (ebook) | LCC BX2347.8.S8 G63 20 (print) | DDC 259/.24—dc23
LC record available at https://lccn.loc.gov/2018006179

Dedicated to
Bishop Peter Rosazza,
Auxiliary Bishop Emeritus
of the Archdiocese of Hartford, Connecticut,
Episcopal Advisor of the National Catholic Student Coalition
(1979–2006),
and friend and mentor to generations
of college students

Contents

Part II

GLOBAL PERSPECTIVE
ON CATHOLIC STUDENT COMMUNITIES

Part III

CATHOLIC STUDENT COMMUNITIES IN THE UNITED STATES

Appendixes

RESOURCES FOR SMALL STUDENT GROUPS

Acknowledgments

As with the student communities highlighted in these pages, this book is the result of collaboration among many voices. We would like to thank all those who contributed to the project. We are most grateful to the many authors who shared their stories, often with a short deadline.

We are grateful to the Healey Family Foundation for its support of this project and many other efforts aimed at building the church in the United States and globally.

Thank you to Orbis Books and the wider Maryknoll family. It is a real privilege to work with such dedicated editorial and publishing staff, including Robert Ellsberg, Jill O'Brien, Jim Keane (now at America Media), and Bernadette Price. The church owes much to their efforts. We are also thankful for the support of the Orbis advisory board, whose members include Robert Ambrose; Janet Carroll, MM; Elizabeth Donnelly; Raymond Finch, MM; Nonie Gutzler; Robert Jalbert, MM; Stephen Judd, MM; James Kroeger, MM; and Sam Stanton.

Both of us have been touched in our own lives by the power of student communities and the work of dedicated chaplains. Our most formative relationships and experiences come from our participation in the International Movement of Catholic Students–Pax Romana, and its national affiliate in the United States, the National Catholic Student Coalition. Our friends from this student movement are far too numerous to list and span dozens of countries.

We also wish to thank the many campus ministers and chaplains who have modeled to us what it means to be a church on campus. We are most grateful to those men and women, lay and religious, who have dedicated their lives to serving the student church as chaplains and campus ministers. Some of those who have touched our own lives include K. Amal, SJ; Lionel Bouffard, MM; Joseph Currie, SJ; Mike Deeb, OP; Jojo Fung, SJ; Luis María Goicoechea; Lois Harr; Henry Jerome, SJ; Fratern Masawe, SJ; Chris McCoy; Mary Sweeney, SC; Etienne Triaille, SJ; Jack Ryan; Melanie Ahern; Mary Ann Barrett, OP; and Kim Zitzner.

Thank you to the Catholic Campus Ministry Association and its executive director, Michael St. Pierre. CCMA is a pillar of support for small groups in the United States. Thank you also to the many students, campus ministers, and experts who served as conversation partners in this project, including Barbara Humphrey McCrabb of the United States Conference of Catholic Bishops; and Dee Bernhardt, Grant Freeman, and Claire Holkenbrink of Purdue University. We are also grateful to America Media and the Maryknoll Sisters, who offered space for us to work on our final edits.

Last, but not least, we are most grateful to Fr. Joseph Healey, MM. Fr. Joe, who some have called "a youth from a long time ago," has been a tireless advocate for the power of small Christian communities in East Africa and the United States for decades. Many communities owe much to his efforts. His mission to gather, listen to, and share the experiences of young people is commendable. This book would not be possible without him and his support. Thank you.

Introduction

KEVIN AHERN
AND
CHRISTOPHER DERIGE MALANO

Finding God on "The Quad"

At the center of many college and university campuses there is an architectural feature called a quadrangle. Like medieval monastic cloisters, quadrangles offer open spaces that are entirely or mostly enclosed by buildings. They have come to define the ascetical experience of higher education. In many ways a campus quadrangle, or "quad," offers a symbolic representation of what university life should be at its best. Many campus quads are literally at the intersections of the academic, social, and recreational lives of the students. They serve as village greens for student life, with pathways crisscrossing open areas that become places of study, recreation, celebration, and even political protests.

As we reflect on the experience of Catholic college and university students, we might ask, Where is God on the quad? For many college and university students around the world the answer to this question lies in small faith groups and student communities. In the face of a critical moment of life transition, these small communities provide students with opportunities to appropriate the faith, develop friendships based in common values, and witness to what it means to be a Christian. In other words, these small groups, while imperfect, become potential spaces for students to find God in the university.

Small faith communities take on different names and adopt a wide range of methods and forms of action. They are called small Christian communities, faith-sharing groups, basic Christian communities, cell groups, units, movements, Newman Clubs, Christian life communities, and service groups. Some student communities exist on their own, while others are sponsored or connected to a larger institutional ministry, parish, or organization. Despite these differences, they all share one thing in common: a belief that there is value and transformative potential in creating small spaces for college students to gather, pray, reflect, and act together.

On Campus and Beyond

The power and potential of small Christian communities of students, however, are not confined to the quad alone. They have an impact that extends beyond the campus in two distinct ways. The first is spatial. Small faith groups are challenged to go beyond the confines of their regular gatherings and the comforts of the campus. Like any affinity group, small Christian communities are always challenged to resist the temptations to become self-referential cliques, or what Pope Francis describes in *Evangelii Gaudium* as "nomads without roots" (no. 29). They must, in other words, look beyond themselves even as they form close bonds among their members. It is not enough, as Bernard Lee, SM, and Michael Cowan point out, for small faith groups to gather only Christians together; they must also send forth their members in mission.[1]

Many small student groups are doing this in different creative ways. Some are living out this missionary dimension by going out to their peers on campus in a spirit of evangelization. Abigail Ruskey, for example, mentions in her contribution the work of students at Purdue University to reach out creatively to their peers and invite them to join them in their small groups. Cecilia Flores

---

[1] See Bernard J. Lee and Michael A. Cowan, *Gathered and Sent: The Mission of Small Church Communities Today* (New York: Paulist Press, 2003).

in her essay writes about the need to go out to students whose cultural experiences are often not considered by many campus ministry programs.

Others are living this missionary dimension through efforts for social justice. Manhattan College's LOVE program, for instance, is a global immersion project that organizes students to go on domestic and international trips to be with people at the margins. The small-group dynamic is key to the program's success as it helps students prepare in the months before the trip, reflect on their experience during the trip, and unpack the meaning of what they saw when they get back to campus. In other contexts Catholic student groups in India and Mali have adopted methods that include immersion or exposure to get students to see and experience the realities of people who are marginalized.

For a number of the experiences detailed here, national and international networks play an important role in helping groups see beyond themselves. These include Catholic Relief Services, the Christian Life Community, Evangelical Catholic, the Catholic Campus Ministry Association (CCMA), and the International Movement of Catholic Students–Pax Romana (IMCS). For several of the authors, including Afou Chantal Bengaly and Fr. Michael Martin, OFM Conv, the connection to these wider groups has enabled students and programs to grow and develop. For many of the same reasons that people need to gather together in small communities, communities need to go beyond themselves and connect with other communities in wider networks or movements.

"Going beyond" also has a second dimension that is more temporal. For students actively involved in small faith group experiences, what happens after graduation? What happens when they go back to parish life, especially in parishes that may not be as dynamic or welcoming of young adult leadership? Finding ways to sustain Catholic students as they make the transition from campus life to a parish is a significant challenge, as a number of authors in this book suggest. Several writers, including Christine Cichello, express their hopes that students will find or create their own small communities after graduation. Fr. Robert Beloin at Yale writes about the ESTEEM leadership program to build leaders for the future church. More research and reflection are needed on the transition from campus to the parish and on how we can better support young professionals after college.

The Student Church

This volume does not seek to offer a comprehensive account of the state of student faith communities. Rather, the goal of this project is threefold. *First, we want to draw more attention to the needs and realities of the "student church."* In a year where much will be discussed about the role of young adult Catholics—with the 2018 Synod of Bishops theme being "Young People, the Faith, and Vocational Discernment"—we believe the specific situation of college and university students demands greater attention and analysis.

We are concerned by the lack of targeted pastoral care for the majority of college students in the United States. A recent national study, for example, found that the church has some form of pastoral presence at only 24 percent of four-year colleges and universities in the United States and only a dismal presence at 2 percent of community colleges.[2] The task of engaging non-white college students, who are the majority of young adult Catholics, is particularly urgent. Several essays mention this challenge. Cecilia Flores states the problem clearly in her essay:

> The majority of the resources and programs that exist for youth and young adults in the United States today are developed through an Anglo-American perspective and experience. Additionally, the great majority of speakers at national

---

[2] Secretariat of Catholic Education of the United States Conference of Catholic Bishops, "December 2017 Newsletter," 2017, www.usccb.org.

and regional conferences for the young Catholic population are white, which does not reflect the true diversity that exists in the young American church.

Part I, "Revitalizing the Student Church," takes stock of this reality and examines the potential of small groups on campus. Kevin Ahern looks at the college campus as a space for mission in light of Pope Francis's call to missionary renewal. Drawing on Pope Francis, he speaks to the need to reach out to economically and culturally marginalized student groups and identifies four characteristics that should be included in any Catholic student organizing. Fr. Joseph Healey, MM, examines small Christian communities of students in light of his experiences of organizing listening tours around Eastern Africa and the United States. His chapter highlights key concerns of young people today that speak to the need for a renewed pastoral approach to student and young adult ministry.

The second aspect of the goal of this project is to highlight some of the "good news" stories and best practices of small student groups. Our hope is that these experiences might encourage more resources (both financial and human) for the formation of student communities. To this end, Part II, "Global Perspective on Catholic Student Communities," draws attention to some global experiences—including the Federazione Universitaria Cattolica Italiana (FUCI), the Unión Nacional de Estudiantes Católicos (UNEC), and the All India Catholic University Federation (AICUF)—three historic movements of small faith groups that remain vibrant expressions of the student church today. We are also pleased to offer experiences of young adults organizing in Africa, the continent with the fastest growing number of Catholic youth in the world. All but one of the chapters in Part II are written by young adults.

Part III, "Catholic Student Communities in the United States," brings together voices from eight models in the United States from Boston to Hawaii. These are diverse experiences that include student groups from both Catholic and non-Catholic colleges with a general geographic diversity. Sharing best practices, however, carries with it the risk of focusing only on successful and highly resourced programs. Our selection of experiences was drawn after speaking with leaders in over a dozen campus ministry programs. We knew these individuals from our own experience in campus ministry, and we asked them to suggest models and best practices among their peers. We wish we had more time and space to include more of these good stories, and we hope the diverse experiences included here are representative of the contemporary reality in the United States today.

The case studies conclude with the voices of Edouard Karoue and Evelina Manola, the International Team of IMCS. In the Epilogue they draw our attention to the presence of Christ in student communities. Reading their text we are reminded of an innovative statue of Jesus Christ in the rotunda of Fordham University's main academic building. Installed as part of the building's design in the 1930s, the statue depicts Christ at eighteen, the average age of an incoming college student. According to Fr. Aloysius Hogan, SJ, who envisioned the project when he was president of Fordham, the figure was the first artistic depiction of Christ at the age of a college student.[3] While it is often overlooked as students and faculty pass by on the way to and from class, the marble sculpture communicates an important message that the small faith communities featured in this book know well: Christ is relevant to the lives of college students. Christ is among them.

The third and perhaps most important aspect of the goal of this project is to provide concrete and practical tools for student leaders and chaplains to build and strengthen small student communities. To this end the Appendixes, "Resources for Small Student Groups," offer several resources:

- *A Small Groups Field Guide* produced by the CCMA provides a useful overview for organizing small communities.

---

[3] "Inspiration for Statue of Christ the Teacher at Fordham Explained," *National Catholic Welfare Conference News Service*, October 4, 1937.

- Br. Robert Moriarty, SM, a leader in the movement for small Christian communities, draws attention to the value of lectionary-based models for student groups.
- Mike Deeb and Kevin Ahern present two overviews of the review-of-life (see, judge, act) method, which is employed by many small student groups.[4]
- a communal discernment resource.
- a brief list of some national and international organizations.

Considering that most college students in the United States do not have any permanent pastoral ministry programs targeted to them, these resources can help Catholic students, much as in the nascent years of campus ministry in the United States, to organize themselves in small groups and to minister to one another. In many ways there are parallels with the context that gave rise to basic Christian communities in rural parts of Latin America. There is a pastoral need and hunger for the gospel, yet few pastoral resources or priests to serve them. So it is up to lay people themselves to organize.

Attention to small groups can also enrich larger institutional ministries. For several of the experiences of established ministries, including Duke, Sacramento, Purdue, and Yale, one gets the sense of a shift in the models offered. There is a realization that large ministries and campus parishes are insufficient without smaller student communities. We hope that the resources in the Appendixes will also assist larger ministries in revitalizing the way they envision ministry with, by, and for students.

A Rich History of Small Student Groups

Small faith groups of students today stand in a tradition of campus organizing that can be traced to the nineteenth century, including the sodality movement—the precursor to the Christian Life

---

[4] In Chapter 4 Cecilia Tovar draws upon her study on students in Peru to show the impact of this method on students and the church.

Community—and the FUCI, one of the founding members of the IMCS in 1921. After the Second World War groups of students in Europe and Latin America, many affiliated with IMCS and the Young Catholic Students, organized around the model of the Young Christian Worker (YCW) movement. These cell-based movements, including UNEC in Peru and the Juventude Universitaria Catolica (JUC) in Brazil, have played a significant role in the emergence of the small Christian community model over the past fifty years.[5]

In the United States, the student church is rooted in two historical experiences. Students at Catholic colleges have long organized small groups. Following the 1939 IMCS World Congress in Washington and New York, student leaders from Catholic colleges founded the National Federation of Catholic College Students (NFCCS), a group that mobilized Catholic students during the civil rights movement and helped to start the National Students' Association.[6]

For students at non-Catholic colleges the options for pastoral care were initially limited. There was anti-Catholic bias at many schools. In this context students themselves organized Catholic clubs—often with little to no support from church leadership, who wanted students to attend Catholic colleges. One of the first of these met in the home of Mrs. John Melvin on Thanksgiving Day in 1883. She encouraged the students to meet in her home

---

[5] See Anna Maria Bidegaín, "From Catholic Action to Liberation Theology: The Historical Process of the Laity in Latin America in the Twentieth Century," working paper 48 (Notre Dame, IN: Kellogg Institute, 1985), 22; and Enrique D. Dussel, "Recent Latin American Theology," in *The Church in Latin America, 1492–1992*, ed. Enrique D. Dussel, trans. Paul Burns, vol. 1, *A History of the Church in the Third World* (Maryknoll, NY: Orbis Books, 1992), 392.

[6] An excellent resource on the history of the student movement in the United States, with several references to the NFCCS, is Eugene G. Schwartz, ed., *American Students Organize: Founding the National Student Association after World War II: An Anthology and Sourcebook* (Washington, DC: American Council of Education, Praeger Publishers, 2006).

"every two weeks and discuss topics of special interest, from a Catholic viewpoint."[7]

In 1893, Timothy Harrington, a member of Melvin's club during his undergraduate studies, brought this model to the University of Pennsylvania as a graduate student. Harrington gathered fellow students together and proposed they take the name Newman Club, after John Henry Newman, who died in 1890. Several clubs were also appearing at other colleges and attempts were made to organize a national network.

In 1916, the Federation of Catholic College Clubs held its first annual conference. The following year Fr. John W. Keogh, chaplain to the Newman Club at the University of Pennsylvania, became chaplain-general of the federation. Keogh traveled across North America to encourage students to start clubs, many with the name Newman. By 1938, the federation changed its name to the Newman Club Federation. By the 1950s many of the clubs had created Newman Centers and received more institutional support. In the 1960s the NFCCS and the Newman Federation, both affiliates of IMCS, worked together on several projects. In the face of the many changes in the church and university world in the late 1960s, both national student federations dissolved. The National Newman Club Chaplains Association survived as the Catholic Campus Ministry Association.

In the 1980s, the National Catholic Student Coalition (NCSC) emerged as a new effort of IMCS to bring together students from small groups and campus ministries across the country. The NCSC was organized as a student-led student movement from 1980 to around 2015. It organized annual conferences for student leaders and facilitated the creation of more than a dozen state coalitions

---

[7] John J. Ricketts, "The History and Purposes of the Newman Club," in *John Henry Cardinal Newman: His Life and Influence* (Washington, DC: Newman Club Federation, 1945), 93. See also John Whitney Evans, *The Newman Movement: Roman Catholics in American Higher Education, 1883–1971* (Notre Dame, IN: University of Notre Dame, 1980).

and groups at local campuses. In the 2000s new experiences of student-serving groups, including the Fellowship of Catholic University Students (FOCUS), Evangelical Catholic, and St. Paul's Outreach, emerged as efforts for the new evangelization on campus.

Acronyms

The following acronyms are commonly used throughout the book.

AICUF	All India Catholic University Federation
AMECEA	Association of Member Episcopal Conferences in Eastern Africa
CCMA	Catholic Campus Ministry Association
CELAM	Latin American Bishops Conference
CLC	Christian Life Community
CRS	Catholic Relief Services
CYMG	Catholic Young Men's Guild
ESTEEM	Engaging Students to Enliven the Ecclesial Mission
FOCUS	Fellowship of Catholic University Students
FUCI	Federazione Universitaria Cattolica Italiana
IMCS	International Movement of Catholic Students–Pax Romana
IYCS	International Young Catholic Students
JUC	Juventude Universitaria Catolica
NCSC	National Catholic Student Coalition
NFCCS	National Federation of Catholic College Students
SCC	Small Christian/Church Communities

SECAM	Symposium of Episcopal Conferences of Africa and Madagascar
UNEC	Unión Nacional de Estudiantes Católicos
YCW	Young Christian Worker
YSCCs	Youth Small Christian Communities

Part I

REVITALIZING
THE STUDENT CHURCH

1

The Joy of the Gospel on Campus

Pope Francis's Challenge to Student Ministry

KEVIN AHERN

In 1943, two chaplains of the French Young Christian Worker (YCW, or JOC in French) movement issued a call to action in a small book entitled *La France: pays de mission?* (France: a mission country).[1] In the highly influential text Henri Godin and Yvan Daniel raised serious concerns about the "dechristianization" of the young working class. Godin and Daniel worried that unless something urgent was done to reach out to workers, especially young workers, entire generations of Christians would be lost.

Seven decades later questions might rightly be asked about the dechristianization of another group of young adults: college students. Like the young factory workers of Europe in the Second World War, the church, particularly in the United States and Europe, is at risk of losing an entire generation of Catholics.

This context calls for a renewed approach to Catholic student organizing and ministry, one whereby students are empowered to take the lead in their own evangelization. In this task, small communities and movements *of, for,* and *by* students are a fundamental

---

[1] Henri Godin and Yvan Daniel, *La France: pays de mission?* (Lyon: Abeille, 1943).

ingredient in the recipe of evangelization today.[2] This chapter explores what a new approach to student evangelization might look like in dialogue with the teachings of Pope Francis, and in particular his 2013 Apostolic Exhortation on mission, *Evangelii Gaudium (Joy of the Gospel)*.

The College Campus: A Mission Country?

The urgent task of providing targeted pastoral care to students is not easy. Some students are away from home for the first time; others may be trying to balance work, family life, and study. Students are exploring the meaning of their faith commitments, meeting new social groups, and trying to figure out how to manage new routines. Like the rest of us, they must also contend with the pressures of a "materialistic, consumerist and individualistic society" (EG, no. 63).

Recent data on the church's engagement of young adult Catholics in the United States reveal some troubling trends. Overall, about half of "Catholic teenagers lose their Catholic identity by their late 20s."[3] Some are leaving for other religious traditions, but a large number of millennials (born between 1981 and 1996), in particular, are drifting away from religion entirely.[4] According to a recent study by the Public Religion Research Institute, 39 percent of young adults (ages eighteen to twenty-nine) are religiously

---

[2] The emphasis of creating communities *of, for,* and *by* specific groups is at the heart of specialized Catholic action (not to be confused with the top-down model of general Catholic action) in the tradition of the Young Christian Worker movement. See Kevin Ahern, *Structures of Grace: Catholic Organizations Serving the Global Common Good* (Maryknoll, NY: Orbis Books, 2015), chap. 3.

[3] See also Caryle Murphy, "Half of US Adults Raised Catholic Have Left the Church at Some Point," *Pew Research Center* (September 15, 2015).

[4] Nicolette Manglos-Weber and Christian Smith, "Understanding Former Young Catholics: Findings from a National Study of American Emerging Adults" (Notre Dame, IN: Center for the Study of Religion and Society, nd), 4. See also Kaya Oakes, *The Nones Are Alright* (Maryknoll, NY: Orbis Books, 2015).

unaffiliated.[5] In this shift away from religion the Catholic Church has taken the hardest hit, with 13 percent of Americans identifying as former Catholics.

Meanwhile, an active presence of the church is surprisingly absent from many university campuses. For example, according to a recent study by the United States Conference of Catholic Bishops, the church has some form of pastoral presence at only 816 of the approximately 3,200 four-year colleges and universities in the United States—a one in four ratio (24 percent). Stated negatively, this means that over 70 percent of four-year colleges, representing the majority of Catholic college and university students, have no ministry that is actively directed toward them.[6]

Even more alarming is the lack of targeted pastoral care for students at community colleges. Among the 1,108 community colleges, the church has a directed presence at only twenty-five (2 percent), a one in forty-four ratio. Generally, parishes are unable to fill the need, as most do not have robust programming for young adults in the transformative period after confirmation and before marriage. Rather than asking why so many young adults are leaving the church, perhaps the real question we should be asking is why any young people are staying when there is so little attention directed to them.

In the midst of these trends there are certainly signs of hope in the United States. A handful of large campus ministries and campus parishes, especially at elite private institutions, have impressive programs for student faith development—some of them supported by large endowments. For their part, Catholic colleges offer students of all faiths many opportunities for spiritual enrichment. Large Catholic universities like Fordham University and the University of Notre Dame serve thousands of students

---

[5] Robert P. Jones et al., *Exodus: Why Americans Are Leaving Religion and Why They're Unlikely to Come Back* (Washington, DC: Public Religion Research Institute, 2016), 3.

[6] Secretariat of Catholic Education of the United States Conference of Catholic Bishops, "December 2017 Newsletter."

with large staffs and dozens of small group opportunities from international service projects to faith-sharing opportunities. At the same time, missionary-driven groups, including FOCUS, Evangelical Catholic, and St. Paul's Outreach, are reaching thousands of students with innovative programs and commitment to the new evangelization.

Nevertheless, the fact remains that the majority of Catholic college and university students in the United States, especially those at community colleges, have little access to targeted pastoral care at a critical moment in their lives as they make decisions about vocations, values, and relationships. Moreover, much of the ministry efforts that are present seem directed toward full-time students at four-year colleges from white, middle-class backgrounds.[7] The apparent disparity in access to targeted pastoral care between students at elite colleges and those at the more affordable, and more diverse, community colleges reflects what the pope has described as "the worst discrimination which the poor suffer. Our preferential option for the poor," he insists, "must mainly translate into a privileged and preferential religious care" (EG, no. 200). These realities ought to force us to (re)consider what our priorities are in relating to young people.

With *Evangelii Gaudium* Pope Francis invites the whole church to adopt a renewed missionary approach. Such a renewal with "a missionary key," he writes, demands that we "abandon the complacent attitude that says: 'We have always done it this way.' I invite everyone to be bold and creative in this task of rethinking the goals, structures, style, and methods of evangelization in their respective communities" (no. 33). In this effort attention must particularly be paid to those students who are marginalized from our communities, particularly those who cannot afford the high tuition of many private and Catholic institutions. Now more than ever the student apostolate needs

---

[7] See, for example, the related discussion by Cecilia Flores, Chapter 12 herein.

a rethinking and a renewal. But what should this new way of engaging students look like?

The Joy of the Gospel on Campus

One promising answer to this crisis is both old and new. For Henri Godin and Yvan Daniel, the crisis among the French working class demanded a new missionary approach that involved the formation of small communities where workers could become missionaries to one another. This vision, which helped to launch the worker-priest movement, was inspired in part by the Young Christian Worker movement and its vision of empowering young workers to evangelize their peers.[8]

Today, that same vision must also be applied to college campuses. Small groups can represent a dynamic tool for student evangelization. Indeed, across many campuses the most dynamic efforts to enliven a student church often involve some sort of small groups.

One of the obvious advantages to small faith groups is that they do not necessarily require large buildings, big budgets, or full-time staff to be successful. Organized and coordinated effectively, small groups can be initiated in colleges and universities without a campus parish or full-time pastoral team. But as *Evangelii Gaudium* makes clear, it is not enough to have just any type of structure to serve the needs of students. No church structure, as Francis writes, can be truly effective—and this applies to small groups as well as other models of student engagement—unless it is marked by "new life and an authentic evangelical spirit" (no. 26). In other words, effective student ministry, in all its forms, must be mission oriented. Drawing from the missiology and ecclesiology of Pope Francis and my experience with student communities around the world for nearly two decades, I propose four characteristics of effective Catholic student organizing.

---

[8] See Ahern, *Structures of Grace*, chap. 3.

Characteristics of Effective Student Organizing

Empowering

First, effective student organizing and evangelization need to involve students as active agents and not simply as passive recipients. At the close of the 2012 Synod on The New Evangelization for the Transmission of the Christian Faith, the bishops make a rather obvious point that very often gets lost: "The youth are not only the future but also the present (and gift) in the Church. They are not only the recipients but also agents of evangelization, especially with their peers."[9]

Here the synod echoes the insights of Vatican II's *Decree on the Apostolate of the Laity*. Drawing on the "apostolate of like-to-like" as advocated by the movements of specialized Catholic action, including the International Movement of Catholic Students–Pax Romana (IMCS) and the Young Christian Workers, the council teaches that young people should become "the first apostles to the young, in direct contact with them, exercising the apostolate by themselves among themselves, taking account of their social environment" (no. 12).

This insight is later affirmed by the US Catholic bishops in *Empowered by the Spirit: Campus Ministry Faces the Future.* The bishops speak to the responsibility of students as baptized members of the people of God to minister to their peers.[10] Through baptism and God's special gifts they are empowered to be fully adult Christians and participants in ministry. In other words, the real subjects of any student-targeted ministry must be the students themselves, not the chaplains and ministers who play important roles in accompanying them.

---

[9] XIII Ordinary General Assembly of the Synod of Bishops, *Final List of Propositions* (Rome: Libreria Editrice Vaticana, 2012), no. 51.

[10] NCCB/USCC, *Empowered by the Spirit: Campus Ministry Faces the Future* (Washington, DC: United States Conference of Catholic Bishops, 1985).

Since taking office Pope Francis has repeatedly emphasized the agency of young adults in the church. Students and other young adult Catholics must go beyond being mere "spectators" to becoming "real actors." Young adults, he insists, must become "protagonists of contemporary events," going out "into the streets" and "make a mess" of local churches.[11] They must be encouraged and supported to become active agents of evangelization.[12]

Despite these teachings young adults are too often marginalized in the church. This can happen as a result of several factors. Consumerism and the rejection of what Francis describes as "the crisis of communal commitment" present a major challenge in the formation of empowered student leaders (EG, chap. 2). Like all ecclesial institutions, campus ministry efforts face the danger of appropriating a consumer mentality. With such a lens youth work becomes a service profession rather than a vocation. Ministry gets framed as providing a set of spiritual commodities to students who are treated as consumers rather than active participants in the process.[13] This is partly visible in the creeping corporate models of leadership that are adopted by some student-serving groups and also by colleges and universities more broadly. For students, who are often very busy and who have never been asked to take on leadership roles, a consumer model of ministry may be very

---

[11] "Pope's Message to Gathering of European Scouts," *Zenit* (August 4, 2014); "Pope Tells Young People Not to Be Affected by the Prevailing Opinion, But Remain Instead Steadfast to Their Christian Principles," *AsiaNews* (November, 30, 2013); "Rebel Pope Urges Catholics to Shake up Dioceses," *The Word Post* (July 25, 2013).

[12] See Kevin Ahern, "From Spectators to Protagonists: Youth Movements in a Global Church," in *Young Catholics: How They Think, How They Live, and How They Are Reshaping the Church*, ed. Solange Lefebvre, Maria Clara Bingemer, and Silvia Scatena, *Concilium*, 2015/2 (London: SCM Press, 2015): 28–40.

[13] Tim Muldoon, *Seeds of Hope: Young Adults and the Catholic Church in the United States* (Mahwah, NJ: Paulist Press, 2008), 12; see also William T. Cavanaugh, *Being Consumed: Economics and Christian Desire* (Grand Rapids, MI: Eerdmans, 2008); Vincent J. Miller, "Where Is the Church? Globalization and Catholicity," *Theological Studies* 69, no. 2 (May 1, 2008): 412–32.

attractive. But such a commodification of ministry carries with it many dangers including the loss of student leadership, competition among groups offering different spiritual products, church hopping, and the emergence of a "spiritual consumerism tailored to one's own unhealthy individualism" (EG, no. 89). Both the students and those who serve them will be well-served to remember that they are not clients or customers but full members of the body of Christ.

A sense of empowerment is also inhibited by clericalism and paternalism. In *Evangelii Gaudium* Pope Francis laments the culture of clericalism's penchant for keeping the laity "away from decision-making" (no. 102). In some cases young women experience this challenge at a deeper level, especially when they disagree or do not understand the restrictions placed on women's role in ministry. This may be one reason young Catholic women in the United States are leaving the church at an unprecedented rate.[14] In many ways college students can be seen as double victims of a paternalistic clerical culture. In addition to their lay status, students are often kept away from decision making by virtue of their age. This can be the case even with lay campus ministers. Here the words of God to the prophet Jeremiah offer guidance to those students feeling marginalized from participating in the church:

But the LORD said to me,

> "Do not say, 'I am only a boy';
> for you shall go to all to whom I send you,
> and you shall speak whatever I command you.
> Do not be afraid of them,
> for I am with you to deliver you,
> says the LORD." (Jer 1:7–8)

---

[14] Patricia Wittberg, "A Lost Generation?: Fewer Young Women Are Practicing Their Faith: How the Church Can Woo Them Back," *America Magazine* (February 20, 2012).

Without denying the important role played by campus ministers and chaplains, students must be given the chance to take leadership roles when they can. Small communities and their networks are ideal spaces to facilitate student leadership. For example, small groups can provide students with opportunities to "scale up" their involvement, even amid busy academic, familial, and social lives. Students might begin by leading prayers or organizing snacks and eventually find themselves leading the group or coordinating all the groups on campus.

Often such experiences of leadership may even awaken vocations to some form of church ministry or to take leadership roles in other sectors of their lives. A study by the Center for the Applied Research in the Apostolate, for example, found that "slightly more than half of men who participated in campus ministry while they were in college say they have considered being a priest or brother. In contrast, just over two in ten men who did not participate in campus ministry have considered these vocations."[15] If only for this reason it is surprising that more effort is not paid to developing communities of empowered Catholic student leaders today.

Finally, student empowerment and leadership may be inhibited by time and financial pressures facing students, particularly those who live at home, who have children, or who must work to support their studies. Not all students can afford the time necessary to lead groups or pay for the costs of being involved. Here, chaplains and campus ministers can play an invaluable role in serving students who may face economic pressures.

Ecclesial

Second, evangelization with students must also be ecclesial; that is, it must be connected to the universal community of believers.

---

[15] Center for Applied Research in the Apostolate, "Beliefs and Worship Practices of US Catholics Beliefs and Worship Practices of US Catholics," *Special Report* (Fall 2005).

This can be challenging for many groups. For some, connection to the church may be difficult when the small group is not exclusively Catholic. This is especially the case at Catholic colleges where many small group experiences are opened to students of other faith traditions. For other groups there can be a temptation to a type of collective isolation, whereby the group's members fail to see beyond themselves. This can have disastrous effects for the content of their work as well as make it more difficult for them to attract new members.

In speaking about the power of small Christian communities in *Evangelii Gaudium,* Pope Francis makes this point clearly. After praising their work, he warns them "not to lose contact with the rich reality of the local parish and to participate readily in the overall pastoral activity of the particular Church." In other words, small groups need to be connected to the church beyond themselves to "prevent them from concentrating only on part of the Gospel or the Church, or becoming nomads without roots" (no. 29).

For many small groups this ecclesial rootedness is found by being connected to a parish, a diocesan-sponsored ministry program, a religious congregation, or a national/ international network. For nearly a century, for example, the Vatican-recognized IMCS has been linking small groups of students beyond the boundaries of campuses, nations, and cultures.

Being ecclesial also means being sacramental. To be Catholic, small group activities must relate to the church's sacramental life, especially the Eucharist, which, as *Lumen Gentium* points out, is the "source and summit of the Christian life" (no. 11). In some cases small groups may decide that they will meet after or before a mass, or some may ask a priest to celebrate the Eucharist with them once a year, perhaps to be followed by a celebratory meal together. The church's liturgical calendar, particularly the weekly lectionary, offers another valuable link to the wider tradition. It can be challenging for student communities to maintain a dynamic sense of ecclesial identity in "eucharistic deserts" where there is no readily available sacramental celebrations on campus.

Encompassing

Third, the church's engagement with college and university students must be encompassing and reflective of both the breadth and depth of the Catholic tradition. Biblical studies, eucharistic adoration, service trips, and occasional youth days are all important, but by themselves are insufficient. What is needed is a comprehensive approach to student ministry.

With *Evangelii Gaudium*, Pope Francis draws heavily on the insights of Pope Paul VI, who emphasized the integral nature of the human person in *Populorum Progressio* (1967) and *Evangelii Nuntiandi* (1971). The church is called to work for a integral human development, one that takes into account the fullness of what it means to be a human person, created in the image and likeness of God (Gen 1:27). Citing Pope Paul, Francis writes in *Evangelii Gaudium*:

> We know that "evangelization would not be complete if it did not take account of the unceasing interplay of the Gospel and of man's concrete life, both personal and social." Our mandate is to "go into all the world and proclaim the good news to the whole creation" (Mk 16:15), for "the creation waits with eager longing for the revealing of the children of God" (Rom 8:19). Here, "the creation" refers to every aspect of human life; consequently, "the mission of proclaiming the good news of Jesus Christ has a universal destination. Its mandate of charity encompasses all dimensions of existence, all individuals, all areas of community life, and all peoples. Nothing human can be alien to it." (no. 181)

Nothing can be alien to evangelization; it must encompass all dimensions, all cultures, and all people. What does this look like when applied to the life of a college student? Attending to the integral nature of evangelization is particularly important for college students who are in the midst of an important period of social, physical, psychological, spiritual, ethical, and intellectual growth. With *Empowered by the Spirit,* the US Catholic bishops strongly reflect an integral approach to student evangelization as they enumerate six aspects: forming the faith community, appropriating the faith, forming Christian conscience, educating for peace and justice, facilitating personal development, and developing leaders for the future.

For small faith communities of students this represents a significant challenge. On the one hand, it can be difficult to imagine a single small group taking on each of these topics. On the other hand, it would be problematic if small groups only focused on one issue, or worse, if they perceived other dimensions as somehow less authentically Catholic. In a highly polarized political context it is tempting to apply political polarizations to ministry. For instance, some small groups completely ignore the social dimensions of evangelization. For Pope Francis, this risks "distorting the authentic and integral meaning of the mission of evangelization" (EG, no. 176). The same could be said for those groups who ignore spirituality in favor of a narrow social justice vision. Either way, we are forgetting that God's mission encompasses everything; we are forgetting the "both/and" dimension that often characterizes Catholicism.

Being encompassing also means being welcoming and open to the rich cultural diversity within the Catholic tradition. This means, for example, supporting efforts by Latin American, Korean, or African American students to create their own spaces for reflection and support. Attention must be paid, particularly by socially and economically dominant groups, to avoid creating racial and class divisions within small groups or the ministry program as a whole.

Engaging

Finally, effective student evangelization, like any evangelization, needs to be engaging. Fundamentally, this means meeting young adults where they are, listening to them, getting to know their hopes and struggles, and using culture and technology in a way that speaks to them. In *Evangelii Gaudium* Pope Francis, for example, spends time on the homily and the significance of engaging people where they are. "Both Christian preaching and life," he insists, "are meant to have an impact on society" (no. 180). Witnesses to the good news of the gospel cannot be "mummies in a museum" or "disillusioned pessimists, 'sourpusses'" (nos. 83, 85). Like the ministers who serve them, student communities must be engaging. Contemporary college and university students face many pressures on their time. If the experience of the liturgy or a small group is not engaging, many may simply stop showing up.

Being engaging also means being adaptive to particular social and cultural contexts. Forms of student evangelization that work at a Jesuit university in New England may not work very well among a group of students at a state college in California, let alone among students in India. No one model can work everywhere for everyone. For small groups this also presents a challenge. How can they find a way to be engaging but not accommodating to the culture of consumerism and individualism? Anyone who has worked with students knows that the answer to this is partly found with serving food—a method of engaging young people that is profoundly biblical! For some groups this may involve pizza, tacos, and salad; for others, the group might center around coffee like the Agape Latte program at Boston College, or around beer, like the small Ignite group that meets weekly at a bar near the campus of Purdue University.

Conclusion

The fifth anniversary of *Evangelii Gaudium* offers us an opportunity to take stock of our pastoral activities. Hopefully, the attention paid to student ministry with the 2018 Synod of Bishops' theme "Young People, the Faith, and Vocational Discernment" and the forthcoming reports from the national study on campus ministry by the US bishops will offer an ecclesial moment to help rethink and renew student ministry in a "missionary key." In this process, finding ways to support and strengthen small communities of students and their support networks will be crucial not just for the future vitality of the church but also for the present.

2

What Catholic Young People Really Want to Talk About

JOSEPH HEALEY, MM

Pope Francis's challenge to bishops and other leaders in the Catholic Church is loud and clear: Be a listening church first and a teaching church second. What if we took his advice seriously in relation to young people[1] in the Catholic Church? What if we really listened to youth and young adults—their concerns, needs, doubts, questions, criticisms, burning issues, hopes, and dreams? Here are some concrete examples of what Catholic young people really want to talk about in their distinct peer groups without parents, teachers, and church leaders present.

Youth Small Christian Communities: A New Pastoral Strategy in Eastern Africa

In recent years we have struggled with the exodus of many young people from the Catholic Church in Eastern Africa (and around the

---

[1] Terminology varies according to the place and context. In general, *young people* is the umbrella term that includes *youth* (often referring to teenagers and those in high school) and *young adults* (after college, in their twenties). The Synod of Bishops in Rome in 2018 will address the lives, attitudes, and concerns of those aged sixteen to twenty-nine throughout the world. In Swahili, the main language of Eastern Africa, *vijana* (often translated "youth") covers the sixteen to thirty-five age bracket.

world). The number of African people who self-identify as religiously unaffiliated is growing, even though some Catholic young people are joining the evangelical and Pentecostal churches for their lively singing, dancing, and opportunities for participation. In 2016, Father Febian Pikiti, the AMECEA[2] pastoral coordinator, conducted a survey about where Catholic youth and young adults can be found on Sunday morning in Nairobi, Kenya, the largest city in East Africa. The result: "You do not find them outside of the Catholic Church after mass. You find them on social media."

When asked, young people said that the normal weekly adult small Christian communities (SCCs) were dull and boring. "Too much talk. We want a variety of activities." Due to African cultural traditions, African youth normally do not speak in public in front of adults. So, youth do not usually actively participate in adult SCCs in Eastern Africa. If there are no prayers and religious activities in a family and the parents do not participate in the weekly SCCs meetings, then the youth don't see the importance of SCCs.

Thus, it is crucial to form specific youth SCCs (YSCCs) that give young people a specific voice and role and encourage them to plan their own discussions, reflections, and activities. The rapid growth of YSCCs has been a new pastoral strategy in Eastern Africa[3] within the overall pastoral priority of SCCs in AMECEA.

One model is Christ the King Parish, Kibera, in Nairobi Archdiocese. In the Parish Center and in each outstation the youth form

---

[2] The Association of Member Episcopal Conferences in Eastern Africa (AMECEA) is a service organization for the National Episcopal Conferences of the nine English-speaking countries of Eastern Africa: Eritrea, Ethiopia, Kenya, Malawi, South Sudan, Sudan, Tanzania, Uganda, and Zambia. The Republic of South Sudan became independent on July 9, 2011, but the two Sudans remain part of one episcopal conference. Somalia and Djibouti are affiliate members. AMECEA is one of the eight regional episcopal conferences of the Symposium of Episcopal Conferences of Africa and Madagascar (SECAM).

[3] This is documented in Joseph Healey, "Tracking the Growth of Youth Small Christian Communities (YSCCs)," in *Building the Church as Family of God: Evaluation of Small Christian Communities in Eastern Africa*, chap. 13 (free ebook, www.smallchristiancommunities.org).

separate YSCCs. For example, approximately twenty-five youth at the Parish Center are members of St. John Bosco SCC. Filipino Comboni seminarian Caspis Jemboy, MCCJ, reports:

> Each Sunday of the month has its schedule for an activity. Such activities in SCC are: *Bible* Sharing (once a month); Meetings and Planning; Seminars on Justice and Peace including Ethnic Identity; Recollection or Retreat; Outreach Program for the poor and Catechism (once a month). For the past months and weeks [in 2013], concentration was made on the focus of rights, justice and peace in political and social responsibilities. . . . The youth themselves are enthusiastic in promulgating what is good and better for everyone, starting from family, community and society as a whole. Despite their different ethnic identities, they hope for change and transformation towards a better way of life and participate in eradicating ethnicity conflict. The whole parish and other organizations are very supportive in helping the young people for their vision and mission for the betterment of the family, community, church, and society as a whole.[4]

The Fish Youth Group was founded in 1985 in Kisumu City, Kenya, by two Catholic missionaries, English Father Anthony Chantry, MHM, and American Sister Mary Ellen Howard, SND. Their main goal was to bring the Catholic youth together to strengthen their common faith, become strong members of the church, and grow into responsible adults. The group was officially launched on April 21, 1985, when the first twenty-two trained youth leaders were sent out, two by two (like the twelve apostles), to start their small groups following the SCCs model of church. The Fish Youth Group was founded on the principles of SCCs. The motto of the group is "sharing," which enables the members

---

[4]Caspis Jemboy, "Missionary Life and Outreach of SCCs in Africa and around the World," Small Christian Communities Global Collaborative Website.

to grow and nourish their faith by encouraging one another to be faithful to God as they share continuously. At least here in their small communities, the youth have church groups that they can call their own.

Today, after thirty years of existence, the Fish Youth Group is very active. First, Fish members hear the word of God. By sharing and answering questions, they find out how to apply it to our daily lives. Second, they do a group activity to serve the local communities, especially by helping the poor, the sick, the elderly, and the suffering. Third, they arrange social and educational activities for the group, such as sports, music, seminars, trainings, and so on.[5]

An interesting case study is St. Clement's YSCC in Mary Immaculate Parish in Lusaka Archdiocese, Zambia. The parish has eleven SCCs that meet twice a month as the adults' SCC and twice a month as the YSCC. Our SCC team participated in a Sunday meeting in December 2013 in the home of two of the youth. YSCC members included seven young women and six young men. In a frank discussion members said that many Catholic youth find the adult SCCs boring because the Bible-sharing portion is long and heavy, and thus the meetings become too dull and routine. They mentioned that many youths are attracted to the singing, dancing, and liveliness of Pentecostal worship services in Zambia. They urged Eastern African SCCs to use creative ways of reflecting on the Bible and applying it to everyday life.[6] They used an exercise starting with a reading of John 14:15–17. Then participants drew slips of paper out of a basket on which were written questions related to friends and relationships. After a period of quiet reflection, each YSCC

---

[5] Based on "The Fish Group Profile," the Fish Group Blogspot, http://fygroup. blogspot.co.ke.

[6] Creative Bible sharing and Bible reflection can include dramatic reading of the Bible text chosen, dramatizing the Bible text chosen, or playing a DVD/ video version or audio version of the Bible text chosen.

member answered the question from his or her personal experience. An example: "Do you rely on your good friends in times of troubles and problems?" The person's answer used the saying, "Friends in need are friends indeed."

Then St. Clement's YSCC discussed general issues including plans for the annual Christmas party, a new self-reliance project, and a charity outreach in January 2014 to buy foodstuffs and gifts to take to a hospice of disabled children. As a self-reliance project, the group made bookmarks with Bible verses in different languages (Nyanja, English, etc.).

Designing Listening Sessions
by and for Young People

After consulting many young people, we came up with a format for listening sessions of ten to fifteen young people, especially college students. We spent a lot of time on our process and group dynamics. When I asked a student coordinator what is the most important part of the session, she immediately answered, "Food." Another student used the mantra, "Feed them and they will come." So we started each session with pizza, lasagna, or sandwiches. We tried to model being an SCC by sitting in a circle. Since some of the students were not going to church any more, we did not have an opening prayer or a churchy setting.

The format was as follows:

Ice breaker: Each student gave his or her name and said one thing about himself or herself that was of interest to the others present (a favorite hobby or something the student was passionate about).

Read Pope Francis's invitation to young people: "The Church also wishes to listen to your voice, your sensitivities and your faith; even your doubts and your criticism. Make your voice heard, let it resonate in communities and let it be heard by your shepherds of souls."[7]

Opening round: "If you could have a one-on-one-conversation with Pope Francis, what would you say to him? And what, for you, is one strength and one weakness of the Catholic Church?" After a minute of reflective silence, we went around the room—each speaking for no more than one minute.

Free and open-ended dialogue and discussion.

Closing: Invite participants to suggest a "take away."

Our survey of responses has been more qualitative than quantitative. After listening to hundreds of students, especially in Eastern Africa and the United States, we found three broad categories of comments and feelings: (1) about their personal lives; (2) about the Catholic Church; and (3) about society in general.

We found a dedicated group of young people on both ends of the political spectrum. On the right, young people are deeply spiritual (devoted to the Rosary, Eucharistic Adoration, and other practices of piety). An increasing number of student groups are evangelical Catholics. On the left, young people are deeply involved in social justice, advocacy, and service projects.

The hunger and desire are there. I participated in a Christian Life Community (CLC) meeting at Santa Clara University. These were students eagerly exploring questions about God, their faith, and its relevance to their everyday lives. The fact that exams were starting the next day posed no deterrent to this weekly gathering of undergraduates who, judging from their sincerity and candor, took their religion quite seriously. As one young woman earnestly told the group, she needed this period of prayer, reflection, and faith

---

[7] "Letter of His Holiness Pope Francis to Young People on the Occasion of the Presentation of the Preparatory Document of the 15th Ordinary General Assembly of the Synod of Bishops" (January 13, 2017).

sharing to ground her for the intellectual challenge and pressure she knew awaited her in the busy exam days ahead. Her fellow students nodded in appreciation.

Surveys among Youth/Young People in Eastern Africa

Our listening sessions have carefully studied the important role of youth in SCCs. Given the importance of youth in the demographics of both the general population and the Catholic population in Africa, the *Instrumentum Laboris* of the 2009 Second African Synod did not give enough attention to youth in Africa. A single section (no. 27) in *The Message of the Bishops of Africa to the People of God* treats youth after priests, religious, lay faithful, Catholics in public life, families, women, and men. It states: "You are not just the future of the Church: you are with us already in big numbers. In many countries of Africa, over 60 percent of the population is under twenty-five. The ratio in the Church would not be much different." But the message could have said much more. The final "List of Propositions" from the Second African Synod treats youth in a problem-centered way, saying that the synod fathers "are deeply concerned about the plight of youth" and proposes various recommendations." Much more could have been said about the great potential of young people in the Catholic Church and in the general society in Africa.

The apostolic exhortation *Africa's Commitment* is more positive and expansive. The pope encourages young people to engage in "active and enthusiastic participation in ecclesial groups and movements. Cultivate a yearning for fraternity, justice and peace. . . . The future is in your hands."[8]

---

[8] To highlight the importance of young people in Africa we have produced the *2018 African Proverbs Calendar* on the theme "Youth/Young People." The monthly African proverbs and sayings related to young people come from thirteen African countries: Burundi, Democratic Republic of the Congo (DRC), Ghana, Kenya, Malawi, Mozambique, Rwanda, Sierra Leone, Sudan, Tanzania, Uganda, Zambia, and Zimbabwe.

A survey of young people in Dar es Salaam, Tanzania; Lilongwe, Malawi; Lusaka, Zambia; and Nairobi, Kenya, between 2013 and 2017 revealed that favorite discussion topics in their YSCCs meetings are these:

- *Boy-girl relationships, sex, sexuality, dating and peer pressure concerns.*[9] Kenyan lay man Steven Juma says:

    I spent a lot of time going to church, *jumuiya* (Swahili for "community"), fellowship, and all kinds of Small Christian Communities where we talked about everything from feeding the poor to Jesus forgiving the prostitutes. We talked about everything but sex. Yet most of my Christian formation happened in a Small Christian Community. . . . We have to talk about sex in an honest, candid way, and that talk has to start in our Small Christian Communities because we are not going to hear it at the 10:30 Mass on Sunday.[10]

- *Entertainment:* Another topic clustered around fashion, popular music, video games, social networks, information technology, sports, and the use of leisure time.
- *Identity:* This encompassed the whole area of searching for one's human and Christian identity and self-discovery in a faith-sharing context. What are young people's aspirations and dreams?[11] This includes vocational discernment (both

---

[9] In our SCCs class at Tangaza in March 2016, the students (mostly seminarians) were reluctant to mention sex as one of the African youth's most important topics (as though it was not proper to discuss sex in public). Finally, the sole priest in the class said, "Let's say it openly. Young people want to talk about sex." During research on university and college campuses in the United States, the topic of sex was widened to include LGBTQ populations.

[10] Steven Juma, St. Gonzaga Gonza SCC Youth Group Facebook page.

[11] At a workshop at Kenyatta University in Nairobi, Kenya on Saturday, November 5, 2016, the title of my interactive presentation was "Positive Use of the Social Media: Suggestions on How Students at Kenyatta University Can Use Their Leisure Time Better." I began by asking the students in buzz groups of two each to discuss this question: "What gets me up in the morning?" Then we shared our answers in the whole group of about seventy students.

religious vocations and vocations in the secular world) and career planning, job hunting, and the challenges of employment or unemployment.[12]

- *Justice and peace issues:* These included causes, service, and outreach opportunities. In his research, American theologian Father Bernard Lee, SM, makes a valuable distinction about YSCCs:

   Full Christianhood is necessarily gathered and sent—community and mission belong together. I can say clearly that while traditional SCC members (the elder groups) do care about the shape of the world outside of their gathering, they tend to be more attentive to being gathered than to being sent (in mission). Some of us are guessing that for today's young adult Catholics, "sending" will attract attention sooner than "gathering." Young adults deserve some prioritized attention *vis-à-vis* their social agency in the world, and base communities are a way of connecting social agency with sound Christian hearts, heads, and feet.[13]

- *Faith formation:* How to answer challenges from their Protestant friends, especially Pentecostals on the Bible, Catholic Church teachings, and so on. Recent research shows this is the main reason that African Catholic youth want to learn more about the Bible.

- *Fundraising projects:* This included emphasis on long-range goals and achievements and how to be financially successful in life.

- *Intergenerational dialogue:* This included the communication problems between themselves and their parents.

---

[12] Research in the United States indicates that university and college students and graduates also want to talk about how to pay off their student loans.

[13] Bernard Lee, "Young Adults Gathered and Sent or Sent and Gathered," in Proceedings of the International Symposium on *In the World of Today? The Church on Her Way in Basic Christian Communities,* ed. Marco Moerschbacher, (Tübingen, January 17–20, 2012), 2–3.

- *Politics:* Always a fascinating topic especially connected to election time in African countries.
- *Culture:* This included African ethnic-group identity and challenges and pop culture, especially in cities.

Surveys among Youth/Young People in the United States

From 2014 to 2017 I had the opportunity to meet, and learn from, students from the following campuses in the United States: Boston College, DePaul, Drew, Duquesne, Fairleigh Dickinson, Georgetown, Loyola New Orleans, Morgan State, Notre Dame, Princeton, Rice, Santa Clara, Stanford, Williams, and Yale.[14]

Here are the results of three of these US listening sessions:

Georgetown University in Washington, DC (September 17, 2017)

Eight men and three women.

1. Pope Francis's efforts to reach out to young people are received very positively.
2. For many young people, the "institutional church" is not welcoming or nourishing.
3. Many ask whether the official Catholic Church (that is, the Vatican and the bishops) really wants to listen to the concerns of young people, such as in the areas of sexuality, affectivity, and personal relationships.[15]
4. The strength and influence of Catholic social teaching is undermined for young people by the Catholic Church's

---

[14] See Joseph Healey, "When It Comes to Nurturing Faith, Smaller Is Often Better" and "When Smaller Is Better: Small Faith Communities and the Future of the US Church," *America Magazine* (May 24, 2016).

[15] As moderator, I invited the views of the students without commenting myself. But three-quarters of the way through the session, I said: "There is an elephant in the room. There is an important topic you have not mentioned. What is it?" Immediately, one student said, "Sexuality." Another said, "Gay and lesbian issues." This led to an animated, fifteen-minute discussion.

intransigence on issues concerning women and the LG-BTQ community.

5. We have a long way to go promote the empowerment of women in the Catholic Church.
6. Many college students are more conservative and simply not concerned about justice issues in the Catholic Church.
7. There is a real disconnect. Through campus ministry and other activities a number of students find community at Georgetown, but then after graduation find nothing in their home parishes. So, they leave the university and end up in a place where there is no community of other young people with similar concerns within the Catholic Church.
8. Following the one-hour listening session, three Georgetown students (one woman and two men) participated in a fruitful, forty-minute video conference call with young people from Mexico and India.[16] The students related to one another and recognized common themes in their respective concerns about the strengths and weaknesses of the Catholic Church.[17]

Loyola University in New Orleans, Louisiana (November 30, 2017)

Six men and seven women.[18]

Perceived Strengths in the Catholic Church

1. Service to others—regardless of others' faith—is given freely as a child of God.

---

[16] This call was coordinated by Catholic Church Reform Int'l, a global network seeking reform of the Catholic Church.

[17] With thanks to Clyde Christofferson, a Catholic lay man who is a dedicated member of the Intentional Eucharistic Community Nova in Washington, DC. He helped to facilitate our listening session at Georgetown University.

[18] It is noteworthy that five of these students belong to Christian Life Communities on campus.

2. The Catholic Church is unified and one. You are a part no matter where you are.
3. The church is rooted in its traditions.
4. At its best, social justice is well lived out.
5. Good spiritual direction is offered when sought out. It is a great home in Christ.
6. Catholic identity is strong here at Loyola and makes me feel included.
7. Pope Francis is simplifying difficult concepts and providing a welcoming environment.
8. There is a new zeal for liturgy through youth choirs and glory/praise music.
9. Our Catholic men's group focuses on the theology of the body.
10. Small faith communities are a safe place and real space to share our faith and reflect on our concerns.

Perceived Weaknesses in the Catholic Church

1. The church is not meeting the needs of young people, and it does not understand the nuances of each generation.
2. Youth are looked down on and feel almost alienated. This misunderstanding is turning people away.
3. The connections to alienated people, specifically LGBTQ communities, need to be stronger.
4. We need to be attentive to the whole life ethic—it doesn't need to focus on abortion. Separation of faith from acts is found in politicians and others in the pew.
5. It's hard to become Catholic—it excludes people.
6. People don't feel included. We talk about reaching out to the marginalized, but we don't do it in practice.
7. Children and youth *are* the church, not the "future church."

8. The church isn't outspoken on mental health issues—we can't talk about it. We need and want resources on dealing with it.
9. How do we address injustice and inequality locally and globally? These issues get lost on parish levels.
10. Not enough focus on sacraments, especially with older clergy. People participate—but they're going through the motions. Entering into the kingdom should be our first priority.
11. Mass can be boring—young people don't feel included. It needs to be more personalized.

Recommendations

1. Make the church more accessible and simplify the language to make the message more relatable.
2. Use social media more.
3. Follow up on the questions in our RCIA sessions. Face challenging questions about faith.
4. Where are the young people today? Lack of time is not a good excuse. Mass is a sacrifice.
5. We have to respond to the changing role of women.
6. We need to deal with the stress of college life.
7. The Catholic Church must face issues of immigration, poverty, and racism.
8. Make minorities feel comfortable in the Catholic Church.[19]

Before the one-hour listening session, there was a fruitful, forty-minute video conference call with young people from India, Kenya, and Pakistan.

---

[19] With thanks to Diane Blair, a Catholic lay woman and the manager of Admissions and Campus Services at the Loyola Institute for Ministry, Loyola University, New Orleans. She helped to facilitate our listening session at Loyola University.

Academy of the Sacred Heart in New Orleans (November 27–28, 2017)

As another type of listening session our team[20] participated in three "ecclesiology" classes of high school sophomores (fifteen- and sixteen-year-old girls) at the Academy of the Sacred Heart in New Orleans. While sitting in a circle and discussing our faith and life, we handed out pieces of paper and asked the students to write down a topic they would like to discuss in their peer groups—without teachers, parents, or other adults present. Topics suggested included the following:

- Balancing church activities and other activities.
- Body image and what beauty means. How to respect your body.
- Handling rude adults.
- Helping the needy.
- How they can help the community as youth.
- How to get closer to God.
- How to make major decisions in life.
- Impact God has on young people.
- Peer pressure.
- Personal relationships.
- Pressure of exams.
- Service to others.
- Time management.[21]

It was striking how many students appreciated these listening sessions and being asked what they would like to talk about. Some other notable listening sessions include the following.

---

[20] Father Lawrence Murori, a Kenyan priest; Mr. Alloys Nyakundi, a Kenyan lay man; and myself.

[21] With thanks to Alloys Nyakundi.

Consultation in Washington, DC

In response to Pope Francis's invitation, some consultation sessions have been organized by the hierarchy. American Cardinal Donald Wuerl, archbishop of Washington, DC, recently organized listening sessions and an online survey as part of the preparation for the October 2018 Synod. The responses showed some common areas of concern:

- Many young adults feel the pressures of a secularized world, particularly in the area of human sexuality, and a lack of community and authentic friendships in their lives.
- Many young adults also feel the pressures of heavy debts and managing finances.
- When asked to talk about where they find meaning in their lives, both Catholic and non-Catholics spoke of the importance of service experiences.
- Young people who make the Catholic Church a part of their life value the invitation and initiation into the experience of personal prayer, those adults who seem "authentic," and the opportunity they have for spiritual direction and help with discernment.[22]

Consultation in Rome

Some Americans took part in a session in Rome: Twenty people under the age of thirty-five, along with seventy theologians, priests, and academics, met September 11–15, 2017, as part of the preparatory process for the 2018 Synod of Bishops. One report on the meeting stated:

---

[22] "A Listening Church and Helping Young People in Vocational Discernment," blog by Cardinal Donald Wuerl, June 10, 2017.

Several young people who attended the seminar urged the Vatican and the bishops themselves to be open to listening to youth talk and ask questions about love, sex and sexuality. A "big gap" exists between the concerns young people want to talk about and the issues most bishops are comfortable discussing, said Therese Hargot, who describes herself as a philosopher and psychologist.

Cardinal Lorenzo Baldisseri, secretary-general of the Synod of Bishops, said he wanted to hear from young adults and experts about the challenges young people are facing in the church and society. The cardinal's office planned a dozen long, formal talks on subjects including "the search for identity," political commitment, planning for the future, technology, and transcendence. But Hargot, who leads sex education programs at Catholic schools in Paris, told the gathering, "It's surprising we are looking at politics, economics, etc., but not at sexuality and affectivity, which are very important topics for young people. Young people want to talk about sexuality and love. They love learning about the theology of the body, a term referring to St. John Paul II's approach to sex and sexuality. I don't know why no one here is speaking about love. It's amazing."[23]

All these examples, listening sessions, and case studies have to be read and reflected on in light of the findings of more systematic professional research and evaluations carried out in the United States. An outstanding example is the survey of more than four thousand Catholic campus ministers and students at US colleges in 2017, commissioned by the United States Bishops' Secretariat of Catholic Education. Of the 1,911 active campus ministers nationally identified, representing 816 campuses, 1,047 responded,

---

[23] Summary of Cindy Wooden, "Don't Be Embarrassed to Talk about Sex, Youth Tell Vatican Officials," *Catholic News Service* (September 13, 2017).

a response rate of 57 percent. The student survey reached 3,336 students. Survey results were released in October 2017.

The survey showed that both the ministers and the students generally like what's happening in their campus-ministry setting. Campus ministers reported that among personal activities, Bible study and reconciliation stand apart from other activities as contributing to students' growth in faith. Mass, retreats, small groups,[24] and one-on-one mentoring are more significant than social events, catechesis and sacramental preparation, and men's and women's groups.

A majority of students do service or charitable work on at least a quarterly basis. Close to 40 percent are involved on a monthly basis in leadership development. Nearly half are involved weekly with social events or small groups.

Students reported personal struggles over two broad categories. In the area of self-orientation, they included self-worth, mental health, lack of purpose, gender identity, divorce and blended families, and how to pray. In the area of social and moral issues, they reported living faithfully in a "hookup culture" and weighed in on such issues as pornography, abortion, racial and LGBTQ discrimination, sexual assault, and the role of women in the church.

Pornography and mental health were two areas where students said they were likely to struggle. The overall percentage of those who said they struggled a great deal with pornography was 27 percent, highest of any issue. Male students struggle more with pornography, while women struggle more in the broad categories of faith beliefs and self-orientation.[25]

---

[24] A valuable resource is *Small Groups Field Guide: A Smarter Way to Build Your Small Groups Program,* produced by Michael St. Pierre and the CCMA in the United States (2017).

[25] Summarized from Mark Pattison, "Porn, Mental Health Are Top Challenges Faced by Collegians," *Catholic News Service* (November 10, 2017).

The Way Forward

A big question for students is "After college, what?" Two years ago, I reported in *America Magazine*:

> A large number of Catholic men and women graduating from institutions of higher learning are not finding a good fit—a true spiritual and service-oriented home—in their local parishes. Parish-based Small Faith Communities for young adults are a rarity in the US. Some graduates manage to find sustenance in alumni-based YSCCs. Some participate in Theology on Tap, a program of lectures and discussion on current topics of religion and theology sponsored by local Catholic dioceses and notable for its venue, normally a bar or restaurant. Others connect with a variety of programs answering the Catholic Church's call for a new evangelization such as the Fellowship of Catholic University Students (FOCUS), Evangelical Catholic and St. Paul's Outreach. The ESTEEM (Engaging Students to Enliven the Ecclesial Mission) program, for its part, prepares young men and women for leadership roles in parishes after college. Still other graduates gravitate to Small Bible Study Groups in Protestant churches.[26]

Our ongoing research reveals that a certain number of college graduates and young adults desire, even hunger for, some kind of faith-sharing experience connected to their daily life, often built around Bible sharing. So, one pastoral solution is to promote small faith sharing communities for college graduates that are either parish based or organized through some other network.

It is essential for young adults to be free to express their ideas. One challenge is to prevent an innovative program like Theol-

---

[26] Healey, "When It Comes to Nurturing Faith, Smaller Is Often Better," and "When Smaller Is Better: Small Faith Communities and the Future of the US Church."

ogy on Tap from becoming a one-way discussion with an adult speaker (like a bishop) talking to thirty or fifty young adults in a bar or hall. Process is important. The young adults should be able to speak. The older people should listen. If during the session the young adults break out into small faith-sharing communities, there can be even more interaction and dialogue. Justice Café is a similar interactive ministry for young adults.

Pope Francis has invited Christian and non-Christian young people from around the world to a pre-synod meeting in preparation for the Synod of Bishops in October 2018. He has said that the March 19–24, 2018, meeting in Rome will be an opportunity for the church to listen to the hopes and concerns of young men and women. "Through this journey, the church wants to listen to the voices, the sensibilities, the faith as well as the doubts and criticisms of young people. We must listen to young people."[27]

---

[27] Pope Francis, in Junno Arocho Esteves, "Pope Announces Pre-Synod Meeting to Listen to Youths' Hopes, Doubts," *CNS News* (October 4, 2017).

Part II

GLOBAL PERSPECTIVE ON CATHOLIC STUDENT COMMUNITIES

3

The Church in the University and the University in the Church

The Federazione Universitaria Cattolica Italiana

GABRIELLA SERRA AND LUIGI SANTORO

The Federazione Universitaria Cattolica Italiana—FUCI—is an ecclesial movement of university students in Italy in which students, during their years of study and formation, seek to grow together in a path of faith and cultural development. FUCI can also be understood in another way through the individual words of its name.

Federazione (federation)—it is a lively organization, with a beating heart of local small groups of students across Italy that share a common spirituality and style. Each group seeks to contribute in its own way to the life of the university, region, and local church where its members live and study. It is a bottom-up movement.

Universitaria (university)—it is composed of university students who find themselves engaged in the university. Here, the sense of university means both the physical place where students learn and a place to explore the horizons of meaning. It is a place of study, but it is also a place where students live, where they receive their formation. The university is not just a distributor of concepts, but a place and time for human growth. The university is the closest institution to a student's life. Students take interest in it and care about what goes on in it, not only through reading and reflections, but through active participation. University students are themselves the animators of the groups. FUCI members are active participants and not simply passive consumers of information. The small groups use a method proper to their role as university students—research, listening to all points of view, and verification of data. FUCI groups offer students the opportunity to think critically and to go beyond cliches.

Cattolica (Catholic)—it is a lay movement with a mission to witness to the gospel and evangelize the university and society. The work of local FUCI groups stimulates the dialogue between the church and the world on specific topics through theological and cultural reflection. As a student movement, FUCI sees itself as bridging the student world with the church. FUCI brings the church into the university, but it also brings the university into the church. And the explicitly Catholic identity of FUCI does not inhibit the participation of students who do not share the same path of faith.

Italiana (Italian)—it concerns itself with the challenges that Italy faces in contemporary times. FUCI groups do not run away from hard political and social questions. Rather, they discuss, analyze, and reflect on the realities facing society in light of the Catholic tradition. While discussing the social and political problems facing Italy, FUCI encourages students to adopt a global perspective that considers the challenges of globalization and interdependence. FUCI aims to train citizens who can make choices and adopt responsible citizenship, whatever their field of work. Local groups, while respecting the autonomous nature of each group, have the opportunity to learn and to "think politics."

History

FUCI was established in 1896 when several local groups of Catholic university students joined together to share their experiences, their culture, and their social and political commitment while strengthening their faith. Its method and way of analyzing the areas of faith, politics, and intellectual life have contributed to the formation of leaders at the intersection of these areas. Over the past century FUCI has been at the vanguard of many important moments in the life of Italian politics and in the life of the church. At least eight presidents and prime ministers of the Italian Republic, including the current Italian president, were formed as members or leaders of FUCI.[1] Aldo Moro, for example, who was prime minister of the Italian Republic in the 1970s, and who was kidnapped and murdered by the Red Brigades in 1978, served as national president of FUCI.

FUCI has also contributed much to the life of the church. FUCI members and alumni participated actively at the Second Vatican Council. Many bishops and cardinals worked as chaplains to the movement, including Giovanni Battista Montini (the future Pope Paul VI), who severed as national chaplain from 1925 to 1933 and remained close with FUCI as pope. FUCI has also had a number of other members gain recognition as blessed, including Alberto Marvelli and Blessed Pier Giorgio Frassati, who is in many ways a saint for college students. These are just some of the personalities that enlighten FUCI's 121 years of history.

FUCI Today

FUCI has a presence in the major Italian universities and dioceses throughout the country. It is structured as a federation; each level elects its representatives to a higher level. That is to say, members of local groups elect group presidents, and group presidents elect regional coordinators who represent all the regions in the Central Council. The Central Council then elects the national president.

---

[1] Giovanni Leone, Francesco Amintore Fanfani, Maurizio Cossiga, Giulio Andreotti, Aldo Moro, Romano Prodi, Oscar Luigi Scalfaro, and the current Italian president, Sergio Mattarella.

The federal organizing structure of FUCI promotes democratic participation of all its members in the life and activity of the federation from the local university group up to the national president. Democratic procedures, deliberative methods, and respect for rules by every member are precious opportunities to learn shared responsibility and participation. This tradition of co-responsibility and sharing at all levels of the federation helps to create students with leadership skills and a willingness to compromise, dialogue, and listen to those with different sensibilities and points of view.

Since FUCI is part of the academic world, it has been natural for it to adopt a method of research that focuses on social realities, examines problems, and discusses results, which are then transmitted to other institutions. In a world where truth is reduced to a catchphrase or is denied in advance, FUCI's method aims to avoid having a preconceived thesis. Therefore, from local groups to the national level, FUCI encourages students to undertake serious research on social issues and to develop critical knowledge about politics, theology, sociology, and other fields. FUCI publishes a national journal called *Ricerca* (research) that includes student research and articles related to church, politics, and university life. It also organizes several national events, including an annual theological week to engage students in serious reflection on theological topics, including ecumenism, social justice, and family.

Forming Responsible Citizens

The Federal Assembly, which is composed of group presidents and Central Council members, sets national guidelines and determines the topics to be discussed in local groups throughout the federation. Each local group has its own organizational structure and meets once a week to discuss topics chosen from the national guidelines, addressing the theme by focusing on social, political, cultural, and spiritual aspects. Over the years FUCI's methodology has developed and now provides a comprehensive approach to university students—a holistic avenue to understanding the topics discussed, while preparing students to be responsible adults and citizens.

Recent Messages from Popes to FUCI

One of the benefits of being a Catholic student organization in Italy is the relative accessibility of the pope. Several popes have received the FUCI in private audiences for special occasions, including the beatification of its former national chaplain Giovanni Battista Montini (Pope Paul VI). The following are a selection of recent messages from different popes to FUCI. These have relevance for student groups beyond FUCI.

Saint John Paul II—April 29, 1996
The history of the past 100 years actually confirms that the FUCI experience is a significant chapter of the Church's life in Italy, especially of that vast and multiform lay movement which found in Catholic Action its main support.[2]

Saint John Paul II—April 26, 2002
Do not let yourselves be overcome by the fear of professing with humble boldness the joy of belonging to the ecclesial community. Do not confuse dialogue with an uncritical acceptance of fashionable opinions, but, following the exhortation of the Apostle Paul, "test everything; hold fast what is good" (1 Thess 5:21). . . . This service to the Truth must have the precious support of a solid and precise formation, constantly nourished by meditation on the Word of God, supported by those who guide you on the journey of faith, regularly checked on the basis of criteria suitable for discerning the genuine ecclesial identity of an association such as yours, determined to be in full and constant communion with

---

[2] Pope John Paul II, "Ai Partecipanti Al Congresso Nazionale Della Federazione Universitaria Cattolica Italiana (FUCI)," Rome (April 29, 1996).

the Pastors of the Church. . . . May your serene and joyful Christian witness, lived in loving communion with those who share the Gospel ideal in other ecclesial groups as well, help everyone to encounter the person of Jesus.[3]

Benedict XVI—November 9, 2007
How can one fail to recognize that FUCI has contributed to the formation of entire generations of exemplary Christians, who have been able to transform the Gospel *into* life and *with* life, committing themselves on the cultural, civil, social, and ecclesial levels? . . . And you, both at the recent Congresses and on the pages of the *Ricerca* journal, are constantly concerned with the new configuration of academic studies, the relative legislative modifications, the topic of student participation and the ways in which the global dynamics of communication affect formation and the transmission of knowledge. . . .

It is precisely in this environment that FUCI can fully express even today its original and ever-current charism: the convinced witness of the "possible friendship" between intelligence and faith, which implies the ceaseless effort to unite maturation in faith with growth in studies and the acquisition of scientific knowledge. . . . It is possible, precisely during the university years and thanks to them, to realize an authentic human, scientific and spiritual maturation. . . . Study constitutes a providential opportunity to advance on the journey of faith, because a well-cultivated intelligence opens the heart of man to listen to the voice of God, emphasizing the importance of discernment and humility. . . . The university years are therefore a training ground for convinced and courageous Gospel witness."[4]

---

[3] Pope John Paul II, "Message to the Young People of the Italian Catholic University Federation—FUCI," Rome (April 26, 2002).

[4] Benedict XVI, "To Members of the Italian Catholic University Federation (FUCI)," November 9, 2007.

Francis—October 14, 2014

Do not be content with partial truths or reassuring illusions, but through study embrace an ever fuller understanding of reality. In order to do this it is necessary to listen with humility and to gaze with foresight. Studying is not taking possession of reality in order to manipulate it, but allowing it to speak to us and to reveal something to us, very often even about ourselves; and reality does not allow itself to be understood without the willingness to refine one's perspective, to look at it with new eyes. . . .

Study and keeping watch, form the true quantum leap that happens at university, which causes us to develop a unified character and causes us to become adults in intellectual life as in spiritual life. . . . May the FUCI always experience the humility of research, that attitude of silent welcoming of the unknown, of the stranger, of the other and demonstrate one's openness and willingness to walk with all those who are driven by a restless tension toward the Truth, believers and non believers, foreigners and the marginalized. . . . Let your method of study be research, dialogue, and comparison. . . .

The university is a frontier which awaits you, a periphery in which to welcome and attend to man's existential poverty. Poverty in relationships, in human growth, tend to fill heads without creating a shared community plan, a common goal, an honest brotherhood. . . . Never set up barriers which, in seeking to defend the border, prevent the encounter with the Lord. . . . I exhort you to continue to bring the Gospel into the University and culture into the Church![5]

---

[5] Pope Francis, "Message of the Holy Father to the Italian Catholic Federation of University Students (FUCI)," Rome (October 14, 2014).

4

The Spiritual Adventure of the Unión Nacional de Estudiantes Católicos Peru

CECILIA TOVAR S.

Initial Years of UNEC

When a group of students created the nucleus of the Unión Nacional de Estudiantes Católicos (UNEC), the National Catholic Student Union, in August 1941, they were guided by a central mission: to announce the gospel in the university by creating student communities for formation and solidarity. The legacy of this simple mission by a group of students is impressive, as it, among other things, contributed greatly to the renewal of theology that came to be known as liberation theology. UNEC has generated a history, a process of searching for the concrete message of Jesus, and a truly collective spiritual adventure that has shaped generations of students.

Parts of this essay are adapted from an article written by the author for the magazine *Páginas* to mark the fiftieth anniversary of UNEC (October 1991); the organization is now seventy-five years old. Translation by Nicolás Cabrera, MA, of St. John's University, New York.

Participating in UNEC is an intense spiritual experience of discovering a way to live faith in encounter with the Bible and community life. It leaves a mark that cannot be erased upon leaving the university—its effects continue through professional life in service to society, especially to the poorest members of our community.

UNEC quickly expanded to the cities of Arequipa, Cusco, and Trujillo. It was recognized as part of (specialized) Catholic Action and was accepted as a member movement of Pax Romana (the International Movement of Catholic Students) in 1944.[1] It organized religious activities such as Comunión Pascual Universitaria in a university environment that was secular and even anticlerical. Members of UNEC actively committed themselves to addressing the problems of their (student) milieu, but they sought to avoid becoming a political group.

At the end of the 1950s, several priests returned to Peru after studies in Europe. There they had been exposed to movements of Catholic renewal theology, biblical study, and the liturgy.[2] It was then that Fr. Gustavo Gutiérrez was appointed chaplain of UNEC. At the same time, profound changes were taking place in the Peruvian and Latin American realities. These included peasant uprisings, rural-to-urban migration, the emergence of immense slums, fights against dictatorships, and political changes in Guatemala and Cuba.

The Review of Life: A Method for Small Renewal

The winds of change were actively taken up by UNEC following Gustavo Gutiérrez's participation at the Second Vatican Council.

---

[1] UNEC was formally admitted in the nineteenth World Congress of Pax Romana in Spain in 1946.

[2] Key priests associated with the movement include Carlos and Jorge Alvarez Calderón, and Gustavo Gutiérrez. They were later joined by Pedro de Guchteneere and Luis Fernando Crespo.

One of the first aspects of renewal that UNEC took up was its methodology: the see-judge-act method, also known as Review of Life.[3] This method involves examining our *being in the world* (daily life as a student, young adult, citizen, and family member), bringing to light our *not being of the world* (condition as children of God, faith life, hope, and charity), and concluding with the hope that our entire life would be consecrated to the extension of the kingdom of God.[4] Central to this method or path is the conviction that Christianity lives in the obligation of *being in the world*, that this is seen as the light of faith, particularly as understood with the word of God in the Bible. It is a search for coherency between faith and life and a way of living faith as a true spirituality. In other words, our methodology is our spirituality.

Membership in UNEC communities helps students assume their lay Christian commitment in the world in both academic life and social life (student governments, groups, and unions) of the university. Community life comes with a new impulse and passionate contents. Each student act, whether in personal or community life, becomes an occasion of conversion. This nourishes prayer in the community, calls for weekly participation in the Eucharist, and draws students to monthly and annual retreats, all of which are common today in UNEC.

It is no exaggeration to say that the impact of UNEC on the life of the church in Latin America and beyond is due to this methodology. The Review of Life has been the dynamism that

---

[3] That method, championed by Belgian cardinal Joseph Cardijn, was described in Pope John XXIII's 1961 encyclical *Mater et Magistra:* "First, one reviews the concrete situation; secondly, one forms a judgement on it in the light of these same principles; thirdly, one decides what in the circumstances can and should be done to implement these principles. These are the three stages that are usually expressed in the three terms: look, judge, act" (no. 236). An outline for the Review of Life method appears in Appendix 4 in this volume.

[4] *Revisión de Hechos de Vida* (Peru: UNEC, 1960). A more complete view of this methodology is found in the work of Luis Fernando Crespo, *Revisión de Vida y seguimiento de Jesús* (UNEC-CEP, 1991). This methodology was first developed by Fr. Joseph Cardijn, the chaplain of the Belgian Young Christian Worker movement.

has constantly pushed the collective spiritual adventure to the heart of historical and daily events and toward the word of God that is vital and challenging. This method has had the same effect in the church in Latin America following the renewed vision at the Second Latin American Bishops Conference (CELAM) held in Medellín, Colombia, in 1968. The vision of Medellín is based on the method of the Review of Life, with the poor at the center. This was explicitly reaffirmed at the fifth CELAM meeting in Aparecida, Brazil, in 2007 and can be seen in the teachings of Pope Francis. In these teachings all of us, no matter our age or status in life, are invited to offer a reading of what *Gaudium et Spes* called the "signs of the times" as we look to follow the incarnate Jesus in history. Small communities and movements are essential to this task.

Another fundamental aspect of the renewal of UNEC was a new theological reflection about its existence and the mission of the student movement in society, the church, and the university. With the Review of Life as the basis for this reflection, students in the movement asked about the meaning of discipleship in the world. From this process, as in the renewal of the church in Peru and Latin America, emerged what would become known as the theology of liberation.[5]

UNEC and the Emergence of Liberation Theology

In 1960, Fr. Gustavo Gutiérrez gave a talk to various UNEC groups in Peru—the talk was entitled, "What Is UNEC?" His talk was based on the theology of the lay apostolate of Yves Congar, Karl Rahner, Marie-Dominique Chenu, and other theologians who were later influential in the conciliar documents of Vatican II. The lecture was about the theology called the "distinction of planes." This theology sees the saving will of God expressed in two planes:

---

[5] See Gustavo Gutiérrez, *A Theology of Liberation: History, Politics, and Salvation* (Maryknoll, NY: Orbis Books, 1971).

the temporal (the natural human plane in which society, politics, and university life is situated) and the supernatural (the religious plane where evangelization, the church, and UNEC are located).

Gutiérrez's lecture was about affirming the autonomy of the temporal in order to avoid confusing Christianity and politics. The distinction of the planes broke with other models that tried to construct politics deduced from faith. Instead, the distinction of the planes promoted:

- the formation of Christians with a faith that is mature, personal, and free;
- the value of proper spaces for prayer and celebration;
- the evangelizing mission of the church without attaching it to any political opinion; and
- the commitment of the laity with other human beings to the construction of a just and pluralistic society.

With this new agenda UNEC was among the few Peruvian church groups that showed interest in the Second Vatican Council, which it felt embodied its concerns and yearnings. The national seminars of 1965 and 1966 were dedicated to the study of conciliar documents, including the framework of *Lumen Gentium,* and reflected on UNEC's role within them.

The national seminars and formation camps serve as important moments of reflection for members of the local UNEC groups. Fr. Gutiérrez, the national chaplain, played an important role in helping to lead the debates. These discussions would be crucial for the evolution of theological reflection. Themes included "Women in the Bible" (1964); "Charity and Human Love, a Biblical Study" (1965); and a commentary about the famous Mexican film *Nazarín* by Luis Buñuel. In 1966, Gutiérrez worked on a UNEC course, "Poverty in the Bible," in which he developed key themes that later appeared in Medellín and in *A Theology of Liberation.*

Ultimately, the second half of the 1960s was a moment of profound questioning coming from the paths opened by the Second

Vatican Council and the challenges planted by Peruvian and Latin American realities. Peru went through a guerrilla experience in 1965 that was quickly repressed—it indicated a great social malaise. Demands for social reform went unanswered. The question arose within the church and UNEC: What does it mean to be a Christian in a reality full of poverty, injustice, and death, and how does one go about announcing the gospel there?

Priests and religious discovered the poor through their work in the new parishes arising in the ever-expanding slums or in the prelatures created in outlying rural areas. At the same time, students encountered the poor in university extension activities such as literacy programs, supporting neighborhood parishes, and looking beyond the university to discover the urgency of the country's social problems.[6] Through UNEC, students became politicized and committed to serving the poor.

The theological reflection that accompanied this process prevented an understanding of faith that was irrelevant to or reduced to the private sphere. UNEC, along with Fr. Gustavo Gutiérrez, worked on crucial liberation theology themes in this critical period, publishing reflections through the Latin American secretariat office of IMCS in Montevideo. These included: "The Pastoral Lines of the Church" (1964, 1965, 1967); "Human History and the History of Salvation" (1966); "Faith, Commitment, and Ideology" (1967); and "Poverty in the Bible" (1967), in which three types of poverty were distinguished. Some of the insights developed by UNEC in these reflections were reaffirmed in the 1968 Medellín meeting of CELAM:

1. *material poverty*, which is wrong and contrary to the will of God, causes suffering and death for a large majority of humanity;

---

[6] The Institute of Human Advancement, which was created by UNEC members and the Federation of Pontifical Catholic University Students, organized work camps in rural areas.

2. *spiritual poverty,* which does not simply mean disregard for material goods, but instead spiritual infancy or availability to do the will of God;
3. *poverty of commitment* as a Christian and as a church to protest against poverty and injustice to stand in solidarity with the poor.

The attention to the poor as taught by Medellín was eventually taken up by the third CELAM meeting, held in Puebla in 1979, which affirmed the theological insight of the "option for the poor."

The Cycle of Forming and Informing

UNEC took an active role in the intense reflection during the preparation for the 1968 Medellín meeting of CELAM and in the reception of the texts. Prior to Medellín, UNEC members and chaplains participated in meetings across the continent, including the 1968 national seminar of UNEC, to discuss the preliminary documents. UNEC also participated in the meetings pertaining to the laity at the national level in Peru and in the Latin American meeting convened by the Department of the Laity of CELAM, which was presided over by Monsignor José Dammert, a Peruvian bishop.

After Medellín, the thirty-sixth Peruvian Bishops Assembly took place in January 1969. This meeting gave a great lift to the reception of the conclusions of Medellín and the option for the poor. The assembly was open to the participation of priests, religious, and laity, along with the active presence of UNEC members, who found themselves with many parish groups, basic Christian communities, religious, and those who struggled with the same worries about the renewal of the church.

At the 1970 national seminar, UNEC adopted the "option for the oppressed" as its way of expressing the option for the poor. It suggested different ways of engagement, including:

- liberating evangelization and the construction of the church;
- concentrating on the pastoral work of the poor;
- participation of the laity in politics;
- showing solidarity with popular sectors and supporting their organization and awareness building;
- rethinking areas of study and professional careers to be in service to the poor;
- questioning the status of professionals in an unjust and unequal society; and
- the promotion of a lifestyle closer to the poor, including encouraging students to befriend them.

In the spiritual realm, the option for the poor was a true breakthrough or conversion. Many students decided to express it by going to live or work in slums or in remote parts of the country. It was this engagement that made up the evangelizing witness of the movement, in which the communication of the gospel is understood not only with words, but also with gestures and actions, and with a life given in service of the poor.

For UNEC, the methodology of the Review of Life took on new meaning after the articulation of the option for the poor and the publication of *A Theology of Liberation.* It was not just a method for community meetings, but also for the rhythm of life in the movement, which constantly focused on discerning the call of the Lord in events and trying to understand the light of faith. God speaks to us in history, such as in the Vatican II call for dialogue between the church and the world. Camps and national groups adopted this methodology, which included moments of analysis of reality (reality checks), prayer, theological reflection, and decisions that make a collective path for action.

The Review of Life means an enrichment, and not always an easy dialectic, between two dimensions. On the one hand, there is the task of reasoning in a faith nourished by a permanent deepening of the word of God, the Eucharist, and theological reflection. On the other hand, there is a search of knowing and understanding a country's reality through the social sciences as well as the direct discovery of the world of the poor in both the political and ecclesial spheres.

A fundamental aspect of this learning was to see the poor as human beings and protagonists of their own history of liberation and evangelization, as affirmed by CELAM in Puebla. In UNEC's meetings in 1974, a phrase appeared that summed up this experience: "We went to evangelize and it turned out that we were the ones evangelized."

In this process of learning and living the insights of liberation theology, the complexity and richness of the world of the poor were being discovered. The option for the poor was not an abstraction, but rather a stance that involved getting closer to specific people and to weave with them the bonds of friendship, sharing moments of pain and joy. Little by little the multiple dimensions of the life of the people, family, community bonds, feasts, and religiosity were recognized. People who belonged to a marginalized culture that suffered the contempt of a profoundly racist society were lifted up: women who suffer multiple oppressions; the poor; indigenous peoples; Afro-Peruvians; women who are not valued and are many times mistreated by their partners; and young people without a future who are tempted by crime, drug addiction, or violence. The character of the God-centered option for the poor was better understood as not being chosen because they are good, but rather because God preferred them, which was an inoculation against the idealization of poverty.

For students involved in UNEC the main consciousness of the popular reality is seeing that the notion of social class is not enough to understand the poor. A profound intellectual reflection is also needed. It was increasingly clear that the project of a just and fraternal society ought to be rooted in our reality and ought not to repeat given models—and that links that bond one's own destiny to that of the poor expect a fidelity beyond the theoretical clarities or successes or failures. Therefore, one lives in an encounter with Jesus in the poor that calls upon the demands of justice (Matt 25).

Toward the End of the Twentieth Century

During the years of political violence that bloodied the country (1980–2000), UNEC found new ways of engagement and commitment: the defense of human rights; the search for peace rooted in social justice; and solidarity with the struggle of the poor for survival, food sovereignty, health, employment, and dignity. Professional studies were revalued in light of the need to find solutions to the problems of the people. UNEC took on a commitment to reconstruct the university, the quality of which had diminished because of violent sectarianism and the postponement of the governments.

In terms of evangelization UNEC members seek to motivate Christian communities in diverse universities, to promote eucharistic celebrations, and to organize talks in addition to the regular meetings that offer a space for Christian formation and reflection using the Review of Life method. The fight against authoritarianism and corruption of the Fujimori government finally took Peru toward a transition to democracy, but it was unfortunately cut short by successive neoliberal governments. The price boom for Peruvian exports led to economic growth and a temporary slowing of monetary poverty. Peru is one of the most conservative countries on the continent, even though the third-place candidate in the 2016 general elections was from the left. However, it is not easy to construct an alternative. The population is disappointed in politics, and the stain of bribery of many politicians by Brazilian businesses makes everyone appear untrustworthy.

A "Countercultural" Life

Being a Catholic student in an environment where neoliberal ideology is hegemonic gives way to new challenges; one of them is the pressure to be professionally competent. But the consequent need for a good education, graduate study, and advanced degrees takes time and money. The community continues to encourage a life of service to the underprivileged and "countercultural" life-styles in an environment where success is measured in material wealth. In the middle of a political crisis whose reach still cannot be measured, a persistent search for new approaches is both urgent and arduous.

The depth of the Christian option taken on in UNEC makes it a lifelong endeavor, not something to be undertaken only in one's university days. That is why different forms take shape for the continued living of the faith, such as the Movement of Catholic Professionals (an affiliate of ICMICA–Pax Romana). Other UNEC members go on to participate in the teaching team, in parish communities, or in the formation of new communities.

Many cohorts have passed through UNEC over the past seventy-five years of existence, and there will be many more in the future who will find there a space to grow in the Christian life. The formation of students committed to God and to the poor (the two concerns of our Christian life) is the fundamental contribution of UNEC, and for that we give thanks.

5

Connecting the Dots with the All India Catholic University Federation

MARINA D'COSTA

> *We were born into an unjust society and we
> are determined not to leave it as we have
> found it.*
> —AICUF POONAMALLE DECLARATION, 1970

This sentiment is still shared by students today who are members of the All India Catholic University Federation (AICUF), a national movement of student communities in India. As I write this chapter, I am thrilled to recall the many little things from my experience in AICUF that have been instrumental in my formation. Being a part of this movement at the local, national, and international levels has saved my soul and has prepared me for a larger mission and vocation.

Each of us at some point in our life has questioned our existence, trying to find a purpose in life. Our experiences shape our worldview, which results in our thoughts, words, and actions. Being part of the Catholic student movement is one of the pillars I have built on in my journey that helps me become more me.

India is a large democratic nation with immense diversity. For example, there are over seventeen million Catholics in India. That may seem like a large number, but Catholics are only a small minority of the country, about 1.6 percent of the total population. Like other nations, India faces a number of social, economic, and political challenges that raise questions of justice and human dignity. For Catholics, many of these questions reveal a contradiction between the kingdom of God proclaimed by Jesus in the Bible and the lived experience of students. The AICUF movement, from local campus groups or units, to the national level, and internationally to the broader International Movement of Catholic Students (IMCS), helps students to address this tension.

Exploring the realities of India can be a tedious task when every news channel or newspaper presents a different story. I invite you to read the history of AICUF through the lens of an explorer. The experience of AICUF is a demonstration of the power of student communities to read the signs of the times in light of the gospel, and to build opportunities for young adults to bring about social change with transformed hearts.

The History of the Catholic Student Movement in India[1]

The origins of AICUF can be traced to the creation of the Catholic Young Men's Guild (CYMG) at St. Joseph's College Campus in Trichy (Tamil Nadu) in the year 1924. Inspired by the methodology of see-judge-act and supported by the Jesuits, the CYMG focused on three areas from 1924 to 1936:

- creating study clubs or small groups of students for intellectual reflection, spiritual enrichment, and personal formation;
- publishing *The King's Rally,* a magazine that was to be the voice of the students;
- extending the movement to other campuses.

---

[1] This section is adapted from C. Valan Arasan and V. Henry Jerome, "Paradigm Growth" (Chennai: Fifth AICUF National Convention, 2010).

In 1930, *The King's Rally* magazine published a challenging article by a young woman student, who was a subscriber. Her article shook the foundations of CYMG. Her article began, "*The King's Rally* is a paper all about Catholic young men, and very interesting and encouraging it is to read of their aspirations and activities, but as I read it, I cannot help thinking 'What of the Catholic young women?'" She then asked about including young women in the group.

It took several years for her challenge to be addressed. The CYMG renamed itself the Catholic Young Men Federation (CYMF), and in the 1930s, CYMF groups were started on several campuses in South India with the support of the Society of Jesus (the Jesuits). In 1937, with the help of the International Movement of Catholic Students–Pax Romana (IMCS), the group reorganized itself as the South India Catholic University Federation or SICUF. In 1948 SICUF was restructured again as AICUF, and it was officially recognized as the only Catholic university movement by the Indian bishops.

Fr. Pierre Ceyrac, SJ, who served as national chaplain from 1955 to 1967, worked with students in developing the movement at the national level. From the experiences of the local groups, AICUF began a number of national programs, including leadership camps and national congresses, often addressing social themes. In 1970, following the Second Vatican Council, AICUF students issued the "Poonamallee Declaration," in which they defined their mission in terms of a commitment to the marginalized. Over the next few decades, AICUF worked on engendering a deeper sense of social analysis among students in the local groups. To this end it encouraged students to get involved beyond their campuses in both urban and rural communities. Small groups were encouraged to go out to see the realities of the marginalized and then to reflect critically on those experiences and root causes.

As the movement grew in the 1990s, a larger number of non-Catholics sought to join its local and national programs. While AICUF acknowledged the role of non-Catholic students taking on leadership roles at the state and unit levels, it reserved leadership roles at the national level to Catholics. In the early 1990s, AICUF experienced immense growth at the state level, as many grassroots student organizations affiliated. This is important in the history of AICUF as these incorporated new cultural realities, including groups of Dalits, Adivasis, women, urban youth, and refugees. While they remained autonomous, these student groups affiliated themselves with the AICUF mission.

Today, AICUF continues to rediscover the world we live in through the lens of social justice by addressing current social issues and training young minds for critical thinking and living with the true Christian spirit of service and justice for the marginalized, just as Jesus did.

AICUF: A Federation of Local Groups

At its core AICUF is a federation of local student groups. It is present in fifteen states in India. It functions at the unit (campus), regional, state, and national levels. This federal structure allows a closer relationship of the movement with local issues as well as the flexibility to handle them effectively. This structure also enables local issues to be communicated at the national level. The AICUF philosophy in social action is close to what Eleanor Roosevelt, who chaired the committee that drafted the United Nations' Universal Declaration of Human Rights, said: "Where, after all, do universal human rights begin? In small places, close to home—so close and so small that they cannot be seen on any maps of the world."[2] This structure of extension to various units in the small villages of India has added richness to the movement from which students have benefited.

Each state and local group can adapt the mission to its own context. Some local groups organize themselves thematically,

---

[2] Eleanor Roosevelt, "The Great Question," remarks delivered at the United Nations, New York, March 27, 1958.

others more spiritually or socially. All of them, however, commit themselves to organizing student communities for a more just society. At the national level AICUF continues to publish *The Rally* and organizes several commissions.

The state level is the primary decision-making body in AICUF, especially with all decisions pertaining to the state. The various states are linked at the national level as members of a federation that facilitates coordination and solidarity among the local groups. The National Council, where only student delegates from various states have voting power, approves of many proposed agendas for the movement. The council sums up the experiences of different states, leading to networks of solidarity at the national level. It ensures ongoing self-evaluation and theological and ideological reflection for the progress of the movement. It decides the topics and themes of national-level programs.

The Impact of AICUF

I traveled alone for the first time when I was eighteen years old. Before then I always had a group or family members accompany me for any travel outside the city of Mumbai. It was my first trip with AICUF, and it would take over a day to reach South India. People helped prepare me to make my way from the train to the AICUF headquarters, as there would be no one to meet me at the station. I vividly remember my mother in tears as I waved goodbye to her from the train. While it was a moment of anxiety for my mother, for me it was a whole new opportunity to discover life. Over months and now years, that solo trip has never ended, and my transition from railway stations to international airports was a quick one. There are so many AICUFers, like me, who requested a passport because of the international travel opportunity given to them by the movement. For some, this has meant their only international trip; for others, this has led to a future of traveling around the world to continue the AICUF mission of working for the "service and liberation of all human persons, as Jesus did, irrespective of caste, sex, language or belief."[3]

At the center of the AICUF pedagogy is the exposure program. AICUF believes that students should directly explore the realities of the society. The movement offers a platform through exposure programs and fieldwork, followed by critical thinking and social analysis. This has been the core of AICUF formation. Practically, this involves getting students in groups out of their comfort zones to experience realities that are often hidden from the lives of most college students.

In my formative years in AICUF I explored villages in South, West, and North India that gave me a picture of what India really looks like. By offering an alternative approach to education, rather than the traditional classroom learning, AICUF pushes students into uncomfortable zones that lead them to awaken their inner selves and raise critical questions.

Getting out into the world to see the realities of people on the margins gives AICUF students an upper hand in their university courses and makes them effective critical thinkers for their future professions. I recall a time in my sociology class when I was in an argument with a classmate on the issues of Dalits. My professor was amused to learn that I knew so much about the grassroots reality. He eventually commented, "She is an AICUFer." Instilling this culture of learning through exposure and fieldwork has enabled students to undertake further research that is aimed at bringing about social change. It did not matter which career path the students chose—they always gave testimonies of how their AICUF training helped them to generate value through their profession. I know of many AICUFers who have chosen the field of law, Indian administrative services, social work, human rights advocacy, and humanitarian work because of their experience with the AICUF program. AICUF has been instrumental in helping many students discover their vocation to serve in social and humanitarian fields.

---

[3] See the AICUF page on the St. Joseph Engineering College website, http://www.sjec.ac.in/associations-aicuf.php.

This methodology has been adopted at all levels within the movement. Students get exposure to their local issues and then graduate to learn about issues at the state, national, and global levels.

Coming from a metropolitan area, I did not understand the reality of social justice. The exposure and social analysis offered by the movement altered my language and my understanding of Catholicism. I picked up terms that were sensitive and sociologically apt. I know of many AICUFers in India from the fields of science, commerce, and management who have spoken of social justice and are sensitive to the marginalized. I empathize with many young people today for their way of being, only because they have not received the exposure that would sensitize them toward the society they live in. Over the years AICUF has enabled many university students to build a worldview that is not forced, but rather something built through exposure, experience, and training in social analysis.

Opportunities to Dialogue

Dialogue is the most critical aspect in the formation of young people. Media in India can misguide young minds easily by representing and interpreting only the cultures of influencing communities and never attending to marginalized communities (or wrongly interpreting their way of life). AICUF offers opportunities for intercultural and interfaith dialogues in various spaces to dispel the myths with which young people live. This approach to dialogue was made possible through fellowship and realized through living with the interfaith or intercultural community, visiting their religious places, being observers to their rituals and ceremonies, learning through the emic perspective (from within the social group), and then collectively synthesizing our experiences on the grounds of humanitarian values and human rights. On my first solidarity visit to the state of Gujarat as a national leader, I was sent into the villages to stay with my fellow AICUFers for one week. That was the most joyous experience of my life. I had all the love and warmth from the people in the village, especially the family members of fellow AICUFers, and I was also document-ing the realities of the Dalit community where I lived for a week. When I look back today, as an anthropologist, I am thrilled to learn that what I did was close to what we know as ethnography. Op-portunities to dialogue with other people broadened my worldview and helped me to see my own society from a new perspective.

The Author in Me

If you ask any university student what one thing they wish was not part of their curriculum, I am sure they would say term papers. It is ironic that as university students we wish to graduate and think it would be possible without our written efforts. While I was a good orator, I was not keen on reading and writing. AICUF train-ing sessions, exposure camps, and other leadership roles involved intense reading and writing. I recall one meeting with my national team members in which we spent almost the whole night in the AICUF documentation center working out the themes of the na-tional camps. I must confess, that night was a punishment given by our chaplain, because during the day we young people spent our time foolishly and did not take our roles seriously.

When we engaged in discussions at the table we were treated as adults, as policymakers for the nation. We were expected to bring rigor to our thinking and our language. What great opportunities to grow as an author, this development of organic thinking and writing based on experience! *The Rally*, AICUF's official maga-zine, is a pathway for students' voices. It is a witness to student expression. As a professional, when I run across some former writings of mine published in *The Rally*, I have a hearty laugh as I observe how much I have improved in my writing skills. But, of course, it is just what a university student in India would write. I also want to acknowledge the students from various backgrounds, those who struggled to think and write in English, who have also made contributions to *The Rally* in simple English. Language never was a barrier for expression in AICUF.

Connecting the Dots

Steve Jobs, CEO of Apple, gave a speech in 2005 at Stanford University in which he urged students to "connect the dots." I want to sum up this chapter by saying, "You can connect the dots only by looking backward." Formative years are critical for vocation, a roller coaster ride that does not always let you make choices. For me, being part of the student movement was a powerful choice. I am grateful to the chaplain who revived the Mumbai AICUF unit in the mid 1990s. This opened up pathways for so many students to be formed by the movement, and it still continues.

When I engage in youth work as a young Catholic professional today, I always question myself, What is it that I can provide to young people that will enable them to create a future that they wish to live? When I offer workshops on dialogue and human rights, I try to offer an experiential pedagogy. My work carries with it the backdrop of the methodology adopted by the AICUF to come, see, live, and experience the realities of the world; to synthesize the experience; and then to create a way to make a difference. See-judge-act. In a world so full of suffering and injustice, college students must get out and be exposed to realities they may never otherwise see. They need to go beyond and connect the dots about what is happening in the world and what is happening inside their souls. This is the task of the Catholic student movement.

6

From the Local to the Universal

Small Student Communities in Mali

AFOU CHANTAL BENGALY

*For where two or three are gathered in my
name, I am there among them.*
—Matthew 18:20

Catholic Students at the University of Bamako

My first interaction with a small Christian community (SCC)
was in 2004 when I started pharmacy studies at the University
of Bamako, in Mali, a predominately Muslim country in western
Africa. I called Bamako, the capital city, home for seven years
during my studies.

I came across the faculty SCC through a mentor, a "big
brother." The community consisted of students of the Faculty of
Medicine and Pharmacy. It was part of a national group called
MIEC Mali, the national affiliate of the International Movement
of Catholic Students–Pax Romana (IMCS). One Thursday, my
friend invited me for mass, which was organized by the community members. My first impression was that the community had
a well-organized leadership, with an action plan for the year, and

every member had a role to play in the community. No one was left out, even persons living with a disability. Everyone was accommodated, and I must say, it was a family. Every new student had a mentor (elder student) who advised, guided, and helped us to build our faith and who monitored our development in the community. As my home was far away from where I studied, the SCC became a family away from my family.

I was elected as the organizing secretary of my community in my second year at university. This responsibility helped to build me as a person, as a Christian leader, and as a role model for other young adults in the community. The diversity of the student members also impressed me. I am from Mali; the students in the SCC came from countries across Africa, including Cameroon, Benin, Togo, Senegal, Ivory Coast, Burkina Faso, Gabon, and Guinea. Though we were from many countries, we shared the same Catholic faith. This diversity enhanced my understanding that we are all God's children and emphasized the universality of the church as a family.

SCC Activities

Some of the key activities within the SCC at the Faculty of Medicine and Pharmacy:

Celebration of the Eucharist: The community has a priest chaplain who celebrates mass every first Thursday of the month and leads student retreats and recollections.

Weekly Bible readings, meditation, and choir rehearsal: These are held every Tuesday.

Organizing the annual student elections at the university: This activity is key because it builds the credibility of the SCC members within the school. It is also a way of enhancing and maintaining relationships between the Muslim student community and our SCC. The population of Mali is 90 percent Muslim, and being part of the student elections enables us to partner with Muslim students on concrete tasks.

Muslim-Christian dialogue: In addition to working on the elections, students from the two communities (Muslim and Christian) invite each other to activities and events as a way to maintain dialogue within the school. This gives our community a mediating role within the faculty in case of any conflict that might arise. It also has earned us the trust of both students and administrators.

Organizing a refresher course for first year students.

Immersion programs: Every year the community organizes an activity that pays special attention to the disadvantaged, the oppressed, and the poor in our societies. Examples include visiting the sick on a regular basis and praying with patients of any religious tradition; visiting juvenile prisons; working with street children; visiting disabled children; and visiting the physically and mentally disabled.

Organizing lectures and talks: Every three months the SCC invites a member of the clergy or a faculty member to talk with students. This is open to students of all religious creeds.

Open conference-debate: Every month the SCC has a monthly debate in which a topic is given to a student community member who leads a conversation. The topic varies from scripture to social topics.

Students recollection: This takes place twice per academic year.

Method

Most of the student activities were facilitated using the see-judge-act approach:

See

During the SCC meeting, members of the group help one another to explore the details of events and situations in order to gain a greater understanding of them and to assess the causes and consequences of what has happened. During this phase these questions are asked:

- Where did it take place?
- Who was involved?
- What actually happened?
- How often does this occur?
- How did the situation affect those involved?
- What was said? Why did this happen?
- Why did people act as they did?
- What are the causes and consequences of what happened?

Judge

In this step the group discusses the rights and wrongs that are relevant to the situations and experiences shared, taking note of what has been discovered in the above phase. During this phase the questions asked to further our analysis are the following:

- Should this situation be happening?
- Do you think this is right? What makes it right or wrong?
- Is there anything that we can do to change the situation if it is wrong?

Act

The group discusses possible ways of responding to the situations described in the "see" part. Actions can be carried out by individuals within the group or by the group as a whole. During this phase the following questions are asked to further our analysis:

- Is there anything you can do, no matter how small, to improve the situation? Is there anything we as a group can do?
- Is there anything more we need to find out?
- How can we do this?
- Is there anyone we can influence to improve things?
- What action are we going to take?

It is always essential to review our action to see if it was successful and to realize what we learned from working together. The following questions are asked to help our review:

- Did we achieve the original purpose? Did it change the situation of the person(s) who originally brought the situation to our attention?
- What difficulties did we come up against?
- What effect did our action have on us and on others?
- What did we learn from the action?
- How did we feel before? during? after?
- Is there anything we would do differently?
- Is there any further action we can take?

Benefits of Active Membership in the SCC

Being a member of the SCC when I was in university was very important to my formation as a Christian and as a citizen in several ways.

It helped to build in me a strong sense of responsibility for the common good. As a person and a woman, being one of the leaders of the community for four years as a student has strengthened my leadership skills. In addition to enhancing my organizational and public speaking skills, it has built up my self-confidence and fortified my relationship with God. As a member of the community I have gained a deeper understanding of values such as humility, compassion, love, fighting for social justice, integrity, self-giving, and gratitude. My time in university was a formative one and allowed me to understand my vocation as a student leader in a larger context.

Through my involvement in the local community, I felt called to serve the students of my country, not just my university. I felt called by God to work for social justice in my country. Even to this day, as a young professional, those formative years as a student leader helped me to be an agent in correcting the injustices of this world.

Eventually I was called to serve for three years as national coordinator in a Catholic student movement (MIEC-Mali). My main objective was to organize Catholic students in Mali to be shepherds of the gospel within their milieu. There is a saying in French, *Quand les jeunes sont organisés et craints Dieu, leur force est inestimable* (when the youth are organized and God-fearing, their strength is invaluable). This phrase shows the importance of the intellectual and spiritual formation of students. We saw the potential of students and small student communities for addressing social justice issues through the lens of faith. Building communities, we saw, emboldened students to take stands for the marginalized people in society.

It helped to build spirituality in myself and in those around me. Every Christian has received some form of catechetical formation, either before or after baptism. However, the standard duration of studying the faith is not sufficient for understanding the whole Bible. There is always a need for continuing our catechism, and that is where our SCCs are necessary and effective. In the SCC we were able to read, study, and discuss together the different church documents on Catholic social teaching, such as papal encyclicals and the pastoral letters of bishops.

SCCs of students provide the space and opportunity to learn more about faith and to appreciate the diversity and universality of the church. In my experience of SCCs, I learned how to dialogue with others, even when we had differing thoughts and opinions, and still be able to live as a community. Our environment was that of dialogue and ongoing conversation, rather than debates with conclusions and victors. Precisely due to this deep interaction with one another, we were able to engage with other university students from other religious confessions.

It helped me to appreciate the universality of our church. After three years serving the students of Mali as national coordinator, I was elected the Africa regional coordinator of IMCS for another four years. Seven years of leadership as a woman in IMCS at national and regional levels has offered countless opportunities and lessons. I have had the chance to work with students and small Catholic student communities across Africa. I've worked with other Catholic student groups from other continents. I have seen the many similarities of the Catholic student experience in very different social and cultural contexts. I have also participated, on behalf of the student leaders from Africa who elected me, at major meetings in the church and the United Nations.

Because of this experience I decided to make a change, to be the change, to be part of the change, to make it happen in the lives of those who do not expect it. One must start somewhere, some day, with a mindset of self-giving and compassion. Each of us on this earth has a clear mission or vocation entrusted to us by the Creator, and it is up to us to discover that mission and to do our best to fulfill it.

How do we know what that mission is? It is revealed in different ways, signs, feelings, and actions. When we look into the world with the heart and not the mind, our ways of thinking and doing change completely, and the world becomes different. This helps us make sense of existence in this world. God has a way of working in our lives, and it requires a lot of discernment to realize that.

God has indeed worked greatly in my life. One thing I have learned is the importance of putting our trust in God, because the Lord leads us to places beyond our expectations. In my travels for the student movement, I have seen beauty, peace, happiness, joy, dignity, and respect. But I also have seen an alarming discrepancy between rich and poor; violence; war; and abuse and exploitation of the weak, the sick, widows, widowers, and orphans. I believe that only compassion can motivate us to take action, and that we need to respond with self-giving love to bring about the change we desire to see in the world.

In my work with student communities I have seen this love. It is a love that is free of any inordinate attachments, including those of status, power, wealth, or prejudice. These are chains that limit one's ability to respond wholeheartedly to any human need, whether a need expressed by a fellow student in one's small group or by another human being on the other side of the planet. The story of the Good Samaritan in the Gospel of Luke makes this point clearly (10:29–37).

I am trying to imitate those who have been endowed with the great humility needed to exercise a leadership of disinterested love, a self-giving love like that of Nelson Mandela, Julius Nyerere, and Mother Teresa of Calcutta. "No one has greater love than this, to lay down one's life for one's friends" (John 15:13).

In IMCS we work to raise awareness among young people, forming them into "students for others," helping them to have a creative spirit, a spirit of sensitivity, and a sense of justice and love in order to better serve the societies to which they belong. Human beings should be at the center of any sustainable development, and that is what IMCS is training students to see. To do this task, small communities, like the one I joined at the University of Bamako, are fundamental for the formation of students into ethical leaders for our world. I have witnessed that God always uses us and has a purpose for each one of us on this earth. But we cannot be passive. We cannot expect change if we are not part of it.

7

We Create the Path by Walking

Youth Small Christian Communities in Eastern Africa

ALLOYS NYAKUNDI, NANCY NJEHIA, EVELYN NYAITUGA, AND BRIAN OMONDI

> *One hand washes the other hand.*
> —UGANDAN PROVERB

What is a youth small christian community (YSCC)? A YSCC is a small group of young people that is school based (either university, college, or high school) or parish based, and whose members meet weekly to share both the gospel of the coming Sunday and their experiences in life.

See: YSCCs in Eastern Africa

This chapter, which utilizes the see-judge-act framework to describe the experiences of several YSCCs in Eastern Africa, is presented by four young people on the Interim Eastern Africa Small Christian Communities Training Team under the Association of

Member Episcopal Conferences in Eastern Africa (AMECEA).[1] The youth are drawn from different universities and parishes, and they came together in order to animate other youth about the importance of YSCCs (*jumuiya za Vijana* in Swahili). Basically, we conduct workshops in primary schools, high schools, colleges, universities, dioceses, and parishes. Through YSCCs, we create an avenue for the youth to meet, share that week's gospel, and relate it to what is going on in their lives. After the reflection on the gospel, youth share the challenges they are facing in life and then try to find guidance from the gospel and through advice from one another.

In Eastern Africa we are participating in various youth symposiums and meetings at a time when our holy father, Pope Francis, has dedicated his efforts to youth in preparation for the Synod on Young People that will take place in Rome in October 2018. This shows the great love, concern, and care that Pope Francis has for youth, who are the majority in our Catholic Church.

We say the majority because most of the Catholic families in Africa have more than two children. We write this paper with a great deal of enthusiasm, hoping that this Year of Young People will be handled differently than the Year of the Family,[2] which had many sweet words and used many resources, but led to relatively little implementation and follow up.

The sayings "If you're going to talk the talk, you've got to walk the walk" and "Walk it like you talk it," are twenty-first-century American alternatives to various traditional sayings that epitomize the notion that talk is cheap. Other examples are, "Actions speak louder than words." "Practice what you preach." "Put your money where your mouth is."

---

[1] AMECEA is a service organization for the National Episcopal Conferences of the nine English-speaking countries of Eastern Africa, namely Eritrea, Ethiopia, Kenya, Malawi, South Sudan, Sudan, Tanzania, Uganda, and Zambia. Somalia and Djibouti are affiliate members.

[2] Proclaimed by the United Nations General Assembly in 1994.

Pope Francis challenges us through the consistency of both his words and his deeds to reach out to the poorest and neediest in whatever ways we understand these words. In particular, he challenges SCC members and others to reach out to "the marginalized and those on the periphery of society." As re-igniters of YSCCs, we decided to create the path by walking the walk because we want to reach out to youth and encourage them to meet and share the joy of the Gospel.

Our team saw the value in YSCCs when we realized that the majority of people who attend mass and SCC meetings are adults, and mostly women. The big questions at this time are, Where are the youth? and, Why are the youth not attending mass and YSCCs? Happily enough, through workshops and other efforts we have seen a growth in YSCCs. The following are four experiences of young people involved in YSCCs in the region.[3]

Kenyatta University Christ the Teacher Parish

Kenyatta University in the Archdiocese of Nairobi is a secular, government university. The Chaplaincy Center is a full parish in the Nairobi Archdiocese called Christ the Teacher Catholic Parish. It has nine SCCs in which the students are the main stakeholders,[4] followed by the Kenyatta University staff. They are examples of campus-based YSCCs. Their chaplain for the past seventeen years has been Father Lance Nadeau, a Maryknoll priest.

---

[3] Based on research material on our SCCs Global Collaborative Website (www.smallchristiancommunities.org), including the free, online book by Joseph Healey, *Building the Church as Family of God: Evaluation of Small Christian Communities in Eastern Africa.*

[4] These groups include: St. Dominic, St. Patrick, St. Francis, St. Catherine of Siena, St. Michael, St. Augustine, Cardinal Otunga, St. Perpetual of Felicity, and St. Ann. A description and photos of the activities of these nine YSCCs are available on the Kenyatta University Christ the Teacher Parish website, http://www.kucatholic.or.ke.

All YSCCs meet weekly on Wednesdays from 6:45 p.m. to 8:45 p.m. inside the university, except St. Ann, which meets on Thursday. Every new academic year each YSCC writes a letter to request a hall where it can meet. St. Dominic comprises students who stay outside the campus; St. Patrick and St. Ann comprise students who study at Ruiru Campus, which is a branch of Kenyatta University. St. Francis, St. Catherine of Siena, St. Perpetual of Felicity, and St. Michael are for students who stay on campus. Cardinal Otunga is for the alumni, and St. Augustine is for the nonstudents.

Each YSCC has the same clear structure, with a coordinator, vice coordinator, Parish Pastoral Council (PPC) representative, treasurer, secretary, and publicity secretary. The larger, general YSCCs (mother communities) of about seventy to eighty people are also divided into smaller groups, called families, of fifteen students. The families also meet once in a week on a day of their choice that does not conflict with the general YSCC's meeting day. Just as with YSCCs, each family community has a clear leadership structure.

An example of a YSCC with multiple families is St. Dominic, which has four families: St. Jude, St. Patrick, St. John, and St. Maria Goretti. The family SCCs also share and reflect on the gospel of the coming Sunday. In addition, the families engage in more sharing of members' challenges and problems as young people. Families also meet at different hostels where the students stay.

The following is a typical program for the weekly YSCC meetings at Kenyatta:

6:45 – 7:10 p.m. Rosary prayer
7:10 – 7:20 p.m. Song session
7:20 – 7:50 p.m. Reading of coming Sunday's gospel.
7:50 – 8:20 p.m. Topic of discussion or a debate
8:20 – 8:30 p.m. Announcements
8:30 – 8:45 p.m. Final prayers and departure.

The YSCCs conduct various activities throughout the semester that are designed to develop the bond among students and with the wider community. These activities include the following:

Charity work: YSCCs conduct various charitable activities, such as visiting residents in children's homes (orphanages), prisoners, the sick in hospitals, and the physically challenged, including the blind. For example, St. Dominic YSCC members from Kenyatta University washed clothes as part of the charity work they did at the House of Mercy Children's Home in Nairobi.

Mass participation: Every YSCC is given a chance to participate in and coordinate the mass once or twice in a semester through various activities such as dancing, doing the first and second readings, preparing the prayers of the faithful, and arranging chairs in the church. Through these activities the YSCCs are fully involved in Catholic Church life.

Fun day and end of semester bash: Once or twice in a semester members organize fun activities such as a dance, football match, or a shared meal. All the YSCCs end the semester with a celebration where they share the challenges they went through and their strengths. They also cook food, which they eat together, and they give awards to their leaders as a form of appreciation.

Visiting and helping fellow YSCC members: All YSCCs organize visits to friends whenever they have a problem. If a friend is sick, the YSCC chooses some members to go on behalf of the YSCC to visit the sick person. Members make a small financial contribution that is given to that person as a way of empathizing with him or her. Sometimes YSCC members also organize fundraising to help those members who are unable to pay their school fees or room and board. This applies to many, because most of the students come from poor families.[5]

---

[5] Also, YSCCs at Kenyatta University have a welfare committee headed by the vice chairperson that addresses not only the financial needs of students, but also their emotional and psychological sustenance.

Fundraising: Most of the YSCC's finances come from contributions by students, friends, and people of good will who occasionally finance some activities. YSCC members ensure that there is accountability, transparency, and openness in handling the group's finances by writing a report to the Parish Pastoral Council after every activity, detailing how the group spent its finances.

Communication: Most members are very active on social media and, therefore, use social media to share daily readings and personal experiences. Two of the most popular social media platforms the Kenyatta University YSCCs use are Facebook and WhatsApp.

In their work the YSCCs at Kenyatta face a number of challenges, including:

Competing groups: The YSCC model of church gets confused with other small apostolic groups of the church, for example, the Charismatic Group, Evangelizers of the Word, the dance troop, choir, Legion of Mary, and many others. Sometimes people equate these small apostolic groups with YSCCs because they feel comfortable belonging to one of these small groups. They don't see the importance and uniqueness of the YSCCs. Hence the different models sometimes collide.

Perception: Some students see YSCCs as a waste of time. They do not set aside time for attending prayer meetings.

Poverty: Most students come from poor, humble families, so meeting their daily needs is a challenge. This hinders them from contributing to the activities of the YSCCs.

Large numbers: Some of the YSCCs in Kenyatta have higher membership than expected. Some have more than eighty members. This becomes a challenge. If YSCC leadership tries to divide the members into smaller groups, some are not ready to move out of the larger one because of the strong bond among the members. To solve this challenge, the larger communities at Kenyatta University have been divided into "families" of ten to fifteen members.

Knowledge of the faith: Because Kenyatta University has students of many different denominations, Catholic youth find it difficult to answer the many questions posed to them by members of other denominations. For example, their Protestant friends may ask, "Who is mother Mary?"

Fundraising: Since most community members at Kenyatta University Parish are students, they are challenged to raise enough funds for different projects.

Intergenerational dialogue: Communication problems exist between the youth and their parents; because of the age difference, some parents do not understand what the youth are going through.

Politics: This is always a fascinating topic in student communities, especially when the discussion is connected to current elections in African countries, because of the divergent political views held by the young people.

Conflicting cultures: YSCC members belong to different ethnic groups (formerly called tribes), so conflicts arise.

As stated earlier, during meetings the members read and reflect on the upcoming Sunday's gospel. Each YSCC has a social media platform on which it shares daily readings and announcements. Based on our experiences, several key topics tend to arise in their discussions. These include sexuality, employment opportunities, sports and leisure time, justice and peace issues, social media, and popular culture.

For the students at Kenyatta University, the YSCCs play an important role in helping them to better integrate their faith into their daily lives. More specifically, this includes:

Prayer: When people come together during YSCCs, they are able to pray for one another's needs.

Spiritual growth and faith formation: The word of God is central in YSCCs, and through discussions on the weekly gospel reading, members are able to nurture one another's faith. Through YSCCs, members learn Catholic teachings that deepen their understanding of the Catholic faith. For instance, the Kenyatta University Chaplaincy has an apostolic group called the Evangelizers of the Word that educates YSCC members on the Catholic faith.

Fellowship and unity: Members of YSCCs console and support one another during hard times, such as bereavement. In addition, members share happy moments in different activities such as cultural nights, parties, and charitable activities. In YSCCs, members live together as a family, hence enhancing unity.

Nurturing and molding ethical behavior: YSCCs shape the behavior and morals of students at Kenyatta University.

Charity work: YSCCs undertake different charity efforts, such as visiting children homes and hospitals.

The YSCCs in St. Teresa of Calcutta High School for Girls

St. Teresa of Calcutta High School for Girls is a Catholic boarding school in Makindu Parish in Machakos Diocese, Kenya.[6] It has seven YSCCs in which, as at Kenyatta University, the students are the main stakeholders followed by the staff. It is also an example of school-based YSCCs. The chaplain is Fr. Mathew Yakan, an Apostles of Jesus priest. The seven communities meet weekly on Sunday afternoon from 2:50 p.m. to 4:00 p.m.[7]

Each community has a coordinator, vice coordinator, and secretary. The typical program for the weekly meeting includes:

3:00 – 3:10 p.m. Opening prayer and sharing of the past week's experiences.
3:10 – 3:40 p.m. Reading the gospel for the coming Sunday.
3:40 – 4:00 p.m. Topic of discussion, final prayers, and departure.

Typically, the students discuss topics that are not too different from those discussed at the university. They include sexuality and relationships, peer pressure, life after school, social media and its impact, unfaithfulness in many families, and single-parent families.

---

[6] Tanzanian Bishop Method Kilaini, the auxiliary bishop of Bukoba Diocese, Tanzania, emphasizes that every Catholic boarding school in Eastern Africa should have a systematic plan of SCCs.

[7] The communities are St. Michael, St. Paul, St. Martins, St. Angelus, St. Augustine, St. Teresa, and St. Jude.

Voices of Young People in the Meru Diocese, Kenya

During an SCC workshop, "Formation and Training of Small Christian Communities (SCCs) Leaders," in Meru Diocese, Kenya, in November 2017, thirty young people met by themselves and came to the following conclusions:

- Youth fear the adults, and as a result do not want to attend the same SCCs as the adults.
- Youth get bored because the activities taking place in the adults' SCCs are not entertaining.
- A majority of young people do not know how to pray and do not understand the importance of SCCs in this regard.
- Behaviors of adult Christians discourage young people. For example, if parents do not go to church and do not attend SCCs, their children will follow that example.
- Youth are not exposed to meeting many people, and this makes them avoid attending SCCs where they have to interact with different people.
- Youth see SCCs as an activity for adults, especially women, because in most SCCs women are the majority. The youth are reluctant to attend these female-dominated groups.

YSCCs in Holy Cross Catholic Parish[8]

Dandora Parish in Nairobi Archdiocese, Kenya, has fifty-nine SCCs including six active YSCCs. These are considered by some to be the best parish-based YSCCs in Kenya.[9]

---

[8] Information in this section is gleaned from the following research material: Youth of Dandora Parish, "An Overview Structure of Holy Cross Parish Dandora Youth Ministry in Nairobi Archdiocese, Including a Case Study of St. Perpetua SCC" (Nairobi: unpublished report, 2015); and Holy Cross Youth Dandora Facebook page.

[9] The YSCCs in the parish are St. Kizito, St. Gonzaga Gonza, St. Marcelino, St. Perpetual, St. Achille Kiwanuka, and St. Sylvester.

The first YSCC in the parish, St. Banabakintu, began in 1995. Later it became large and was thus subdivided into two others, St. Kizito and St. Gonzaga Gonza in 1998 and 1999, respectively. The original communities of St. Buzabalwayo and St. Bazekuketa were also formed in 1999; St. Buzabalwayo was subdivided into St. Achille Kiwanuka and St. Sylvester, while St. Bazekuketa was subdivided into St. Marcelino and St. Perpetua.

The six YSCCs have an average membership of thirty people. They meet weekly on their own, but also once a month with their parents to deliberate and plan for the coming months' activities. The following is the general program of the weekly meetings of these YSCCs:

3:00 – 3:30 p.m. Opening prayers/praying the Rosary
3:30 – 3:40 p.m. Praise and worship
3:40 – 4:15 p.m. Reading and sharing of the coming Sunday's gospel
4:15 – 4:30 p.m. Prayer partners
4:30 – 5:00 p.m. Bonding session—day's topic discussion
5:00 – 5:15 p.m. Closing prayers

Parish-based YSCCs have several benefits. First, they promote cohesion and peace among the youth through dialogue. Second, they encourage teamwork in the parish through various joint youth activities. Third, the YSCCs within a parish nurture talents through sports and games between the communities. Fourth, the YSCCs encourage good moral values through seminars. Finally, YSCCs enable young people to teach one another how to pray.

But there are also challenges facing these parish communities. Members of Dandora Parish identify the following as major challenges:

- Lack of proper programs that can assist young people with securing income for their personal upkeep.
- An increasing rate of early pregnancies among the young girls.

- A lack of commitment among some leaders to provide good leadership in YSCCs.
- Rampant tribalism in YSCCs.
- Political intolerance, especially during elections.
- A lack of attendance at YSCCs by many youth.

Judge: Importance of YSCCs

Based on the above case studies, it is clear that YSCCs are and will be vital for the Catholic Church in Eastern Africa. We ask our pope, bishops, priests and lay people to support the youth in their quest to form YSCCs. In general, YSCCs, whether they are based at a university, high school, or parish, serve a number of important functions in the lives of East African Catholic students.

These include:

- Helping young Catholics feel that they are the church and thus more responsible for church life and decision making.
- Encouraging stronger interpersonal relationships, acceptance of the word of God, review of one's life, and reflection upon our reality in light of the gospel.
- Serving as agents of evangelization.
- Promoting the use of the Bible among the youth—many YSCCs are lectionary based, meaning that in their weekly meetings they use the gospel of the coming Sunday.
- Opening an avenue for youth to pray and listen to God.
- Offering a safe place where youth can meet and share their needs, experiences, and life issues such as sex (romantic relationships), media use, gambling, and unemployment.
- Encouraging members to be responsible and also to take on responsibilities.
- Acting as agents of reconciliation through the YSCC, which can be both a path for and a place of reconciliation.

Act: Strengthening YSCCs

It will be important to include the voices of YSCCs in Kenya in preparations for the Synod of Bishops General Assembly in Rome in October 2018. To this end, some Kenyan young people have filled out and returned an online questionnaire to the Vatican. But more efforts are needed.

First, there needs to be a nationwide campaign in all Catholic parishes to spearhead the forming of SCCs, including special communities for youth and students. To do this, YSCC workshops could be offered at different parishes, dioceses, and schools. Second, efforts need to be made to make YSCCs more appealing by having programs that will benefit the members socially, economically, and psychologically. Some groups are already doing this, and we can learn from their experiences. Finally, more is needed to connect young people and to develop YSCCs through the networking tools provided by social media.

Part III

CATHOLIC STUDENT
COMMUNITIES IN THE
UNITED STATES

8

The Christian Life Community
Program at Boston College

CHRISTINE CICHELLO

The Boston College Christian Life Community (CLC) program was started in 2005 by two members of the campus ministry staff, Fr. James Erps, SJ, and Catherine Brunelle. The CLC program at Boston College is made up of student-led, intentional, small, faith-sharing communities that meet each week for an hour. CLC is unique in that the source and instrument of spirituality is the *Spiritual Exercises* of St. Ignatius of Loyola, the founder of the Jesuits. In addition, CLC recognizes the need for community in living out our faith. CLC is a worldwide movement of Christians, but there is a particular flourishing and interest in CLC among young people at the college level, particularly at Jesuit colleges in the United States.

A recent survey has found more than 280 small CLC faith groups at seventeen of the twenty-eight Jesuit colleges and universities in the United States. While most use the name CLC, others use names like Camino, Spiritual Life Communities, Faith Groups, and Companion Groups. For the more than two thousand students involved in these groups, CLC involvement is often described as a significant part of their experience in Jesuit higher education.

The Principle and Foundation of the *Spiritual Exercises* of St. Ignatius is a coordinating and integrating force for students, inviting them to seek and see everything in terms of their relationship with God, their deepest desire. Community helps us in this process of reflecting on our experiences where we are challenged to prioritize continually and see all experiences and relationships as they hinder or draw us closer to God. Much of the CLC leadership training involves deepening our listening skills, both in prayer with God and with one another. CLC offers young people a vocation or at least an initiation into a way of life in the church, and it can help facilitate a college student's emergence into an adult faith in the church.

At Boston College we have twenty-five groups that meet each week with more than 250 members: seven first-year groups, six sophomore groups, seven junior groups, four senior groups, and a Latin American group that meets after the Spanish mass. First-year groups are led by sophomores, sophomores by juniors, juniors by seniors, and senior groups are led by Jesuit scholastics and graduate students at the School of Theology and Ministry. Each group has two leaders, or guides, who are interviewed and selected in the spring and make a commitment to attend an early September retreat and monthly formation afternoons throughout the academic year. CLC also hosts bi-weekly Taizé prayer services, a Thanksgiving dinner, social events, and a senior appreciation mass and dinner. In February, seniors and council members run a "Beloved Retreat," which loosely follows the *Spiritual Exercises*.

Community, Spirituality, and Mission

The three pillars of Boston College's CLC program are community, spirituality, and mission. Each year one is emphasized more than the other two in the programming and small group meetings. Nevertheless, all three are present in some way in the weekly meetings of CLC groups. The typical format of the Boston College CLC group is this:

Opening prayer (in the form of a song, poem, or scripture reading, followed by spontaneous prayer) (5 minutes)

Highs/lows/graces of the week, or where they see God (10 minutes)

Introduction of some topic or content (TED Talk, gospel reading, etc.) (15 minutes)

Silent prayer (5 minutes)

Deeper listening and sharing on anything that has touched them about what has been shared so far (15 minutes)

Closing prayer (many times simply, "Does anyone have a prayer they would like to offer?" or "Share on a grace desired in looking to the future—an invitation, revelation, or consolation you feel from God," and closing with an Our Father or Glory Be) (5 minutes)

The CLC Council

Key to the structure of Boston College's program is the CLC Council, which is composed of eight to ten students, mostly seniors and juniors, and a graduate assistant with whom I work closely each week. Two students serve as leaders of the council, which meets weekly and is responsible for the planning of retreats, formation of leaders, community-wide events, and other activities. Additionally, I meet weekly with the two student leaders to plan the agenda of our council meeting. The leaders are also responsible for keeping track of all the groups and registrations, running the meetings, and keeping us on task.

Along with planning upcoming events, we try to have our council be its own CLC group by devoting every third meeting to prayer and checking in with one another on a deeper level. The council's deep faith life is often a primary draw to other students to join. I hear every year that students feel challenged and desire to be like the seniors before them in their commitment to their faith life and legacy to Boston College. A council member recently commented that she noticed how we do not really share our "real" highs and lows in our first round of listening and that the process of having a second round of listening encourages us to peel away the layers in order to be more vulnerable.

This council also teaches me so much about how we need to develop as a program. Most members of the council have been in a CLC group for three years and leading a group for two years, so it is their insights, energy, commitment, and faith life that drive the program. Also, their perceptions on where we are falling short help us pray and discern where we need to grow.

Resources

First-year groups are focused on building community. The primary resources we use include the youngadultclc.org website, the enneagram personality test, the 5 Love Languages, silence and journaling with the Ignatius Awareness Examen, active listening, "self-care and God-care," TED Talks on vulnerability and empathy, and more. We also touch on Ignatian terms such as the Principle and Foundation, *cura personalis* (care of the whole person), and consolation and desolation. CLC seeks to ground students in Catholic prayer practices like Lectio Divina and centering prayer and community.

Second- and third-year groups focus more explicitly on the spiritual pillar of CLC by inviting our leaders to make a deeper commitment to their own personal prayer life by meeting with a spiritual director or companion once a month (generally a graduate student or Jesuit scholastic) as well as by developing a comfort level with leading prayer. We do this by exploring more prayer practices both personally and communally. We have sessions on finding God in art (either exploring emotions through color or reflecting on a painting), nature, and music, and we invite students to make connections between listening to others in relationship and listening to God in prayer. Among the prayer practices we stress are Ignatius's "contemplation of place" with scripture. I am always moved by the different ways scripture touches each student personally.

In their junior year we also invite students to explore other faiths and religious practices, in part to learn more about their own faith. For example, we had Muslim students come and share with our leaders about their prayer life. The humility and prayer life of the Muslim students challenged us in our own prayer life and helped us make connections to our own Christian faith. Many of the students then brought it back to their groups or had Muslim students visit their groups. There are also a few Muslim students in CLC. My current graduate assistant for CLC, who is a student in Boston College's School of Theology and Ministry and its Master of Divinity program, Ariell Watson, has also helped develop a series on spirituality and sexuality for our junior groups. This includes topics on the incarnation, gender, vocation, and celibacy and intimacy.

Our senior-year groups focus on the pillar of mission, inviting students to explore a sense of vocation and discern where God is inviting them to serve when they graduate. We also challenge them to seek out a parish and faith community (and possibly start or join a CLC) wherever they are when they graduate. Seniors primarily use the resources on the ignatianspirituality.org website and follow the spiritual exercises throughout the year. During senior year we are more explicit in trying to move students from the head to the heart, to move their understanding of some of the Ignatian terms to their experiences by making a deeper commitment to their faith and prayer life. Our strongest leaders are the ones who are not only leading groups but who are in groups themselves. We stress senior year that being in a group is more important than leading. The sense of mission is integrated in all four years in its emphasis on living out their faith beyond their one-hour-a-week of faith sharing and being a presence of Jesus in the world by loving others as they are loved. The sense of mission is also reinforced in the importance of seeing their leadership as servant leadership and as God's work, not their own.

Challenges

We are proud of what our program has accomplished so far (through the Holy Spirit), but there are ways in which we are not meeting the needs of our members. Some of the challenges we face are the continued faith formation of our leaders. We go on retreat with them, offer resources, have check-ins with them once a month—but some groups flounder, some leaders have competing commitments, and some newly registered members for one reason or another decide to no longer continue. We need to work on accountability and support of our leaders and members.

Another challenge is that students often only see themselves as their own eight-member CLC group and do not see how they are connected to a larger community and way of life. Ideally, we would like students to see themselves as connected to a worldwide community and to the apostolic mission of the church.

One of the ways we have attempted to address these challenges is to have leaders recommit every year rather than lead the same group for three years. A couple of years ago the norm was for a sophomore leader to sign up to lead the same group for three years, until its members graduate. Now leaders sign up and recommit each year. We also have members re-register each year and strongly encourage members to join a different group from the previous year. We are still phasing this change into the program.

Another challenge is that we do not have a lot of diversity in our program. Although we address issues of racism and cultural diversity in our small groups, and we meet with and support programs that address race on our campus, our organization is not as racially or culturally diverse as we would like. One way we hope to address this challenge is to work harder to have our council and leaders personally reach out to students of color.

Probably the most important change we made in recent years was changing the name of our program at Boston College from *Cura* to Christian Life Community. When CLC was started here in 2005, it was called *Cura*. Last year's council felt strongly about making the change, and we prayerfully and intentionally discerned that the positives outweighed the negatives. This was not easy, as there are some who felt that identifying as Christian meant they had all the answers or that their job as leaders was to convert others to Christianity. We decided to go ahead with the name change, and it has been positive thus far. Using the CLC name has helped better connect leaders and members to the rich Jesuit Christian tradition and has enabled them to experience the global community and apostolic mission of the worldwide CLC movement.

Impact

A recent survey of seniors involved in CLC at Boston College showed that a higher percentage of students who experience anxiety or depression are involved in CLC. I like to think that CLC offers a caring and loving community for students experiencing anxiety or depression, but I also believe that there is something about the mental healthcare crisis in our country and on our campuses nationwide that points to a deeper spiritual desire and longing for God and community that CLC provides.

CLC is an active voice on campus and a venue for students to dialogue on what is happening, not only in their everyday lives but in the world. I think that CLC offers a place where students will experience love, especially those who might feel ostracized or marginalized from the church or society. My council members arranged to have students from FACES, a student group promoting dialogue on race on campus, speak to our CLC group leaders. We developed a session on racism and asked all groups to dialogue about it in their groups, to attend events sponsored by the Black Student Forum, and to take classes to understand personal biases and ways we can work to keep the conversation going and work for systemic change.

One student recently shared that, for her, CLC offers consistency in her life and an intentional opportunity to look back on her experiences, and that her CLC group holds her accountable for her faith. She said that CLC promotes personal and spiritual growth and has provided for her a process and community to help integrate faith in the decisions she makes in her life.

As a campus minister of CLC at a vibrant Catholic, Jesuit institution like Boston College, I experience so much hope and life in the church. The support of campus ministry staff and professors, the more than seventy Jesuits and Jesuit scholastics on campus, and the graduate students and professors at the School of Theology and Ministry offer a rich community of mentors who challenge us and support us in our faith. My hope and prayer is that the more than five hundred members of CLC at the university level who graduate each year across the nation will find one another, will seek ways to be a part of a parish and CLC group, and will offer a way of listening and being present to one another that transcends their relationships and embodies Jesus in the world.

9

The Catholic Relief Services Model

KIM LAMBERTY AND DANIELLE ROBERTS

"I have grown so much deeper in my faith as I have been given this opportunity to live out our baptismal call and responsibility of service toward others, especially the poor and oppressed."

"It is amazing that at our seemingly insular campuses, we have the potential to join the greater body of Christ through solidarity and compassion."[1]

These reflections are examples of student comments collected from Catholic Relief Services (CRS) student ambassadors during the summer of 2016. The students were evaluating a national gathering hosted by CRS involving college students and staff from forty-six campuses across the country. Each of these forty-six campuses, plus more than fifty additional campuses that were not

---

[1] All quotations from individuals are taken from CRS student ambassador evaluations or personal interviews. For more information on the CRS model, see information@university.crs.org.

represented during that leadership summit, have partnered with CRS to create and sustain a CRS student ambassador chapter. Through this initiative, student leaders who have been trained by CRS, together with faculty and staff advisers, gather as small groups on campus. They seek to grow in their passion for a faith that does justice, as well as engage their larger campus communities in reflection and tangible action toward the co-creation of a world made new through living out one's faith. These campus communities are forming a national network, a growing student movement of embodied Catholic social teaching.

Background: Toward Integral Human Development

CRS was founded in 1943 by the Roman Catholic bishops of the United States to help resettle World War II refugees in Europe. CRS continues to provide relief in emergency situations and long-term engagement to address root causes of global poverty and violence by working together with local communities toward integral human development. Grounded in the Pope Paul VI document *Populorum Progressio*, integral human development provides a holistic framework for relief and development that aims to strengthen the capacity of local community leadership to be the protagonists of its own development and seeks to uncover root causes that might require outside intervention for resolution.

In recent years, the CRS understanding of integral human development has expanded to include inviting Catholics in the United States to stand in solidarity with the world's poor and marginalized by taking concrete actions here that will influence poverty and violence overseas. These actions include prayer and reflection, education about global poverty and violence, almsgiving, legislative advocacy, use of social and other media to raise awareness, influencing decisions about consumption and spending, and promoting corporate responsibility.

The work that CRS does with colleges and universities in the United States represents an important part of this effort. CRS partners with campuses to contribute to the formation of young people in the United States to recognize themselves, individually and communally, as global citizens with a part to play in constructing the kingdom of God.

The CRS Student Ambassador Program

Since its founding at Villanova University in 2006 and Cabrini University in 2007, the CRS student ambassador program, now present on roughly one hundred campuses across the country (and growing), has become an important mechanism for mobilizing the higher education community. CRS staff members support the chapters through training, resources, and direction, and the campuses themselves take ownership in the form of staff support, guidance, and funding. College students are vital change makers in the struggle for justice and peace, and CRS and its partner campuses agree that together they can cultivate intelligent, informed, and actively engaged global leaders who draw on Catholic social teaching as a basis for action.

An important turning point for this initiative occurred in 2010, as CRS ambassadors across the United States responded to heightened attention on Sudan and participated in the CRS advocacy work for peace during the South Sudan independence referendum. This shared mission provided more structure, formality, and meaning to the CRS ambassador programs on individual campuses and supported the growth of a national network encompassing the three pillars of prayer, education, and action.

By 2013, the CRS student ambassador program was a significant part of the CRS agency strategy, and by the 2017–18 academic year, CRS student ambassadors across more than one hundred campuses see themselves as "more than just another student group." They understand, and articulate, that their efforts as intentional communities on campus have given them "confidence that we can make a change." Ambassador chapters usually elect officers, hold regular meetings, and are institutionalized to become part of campus life. CRS holds regional trainings at the start of each academic year and a leadership conference every other year.

The CRS student ambassador movement is currently organized around this message: "I am the cause. I am the solution." "I am the cause" reflects a spirituality that understands the self as part of the larger human family created in God's image, and so the actions of one affect not just the self but the community and world. Students are invited to take personal responsibility for the suffering of others. "I am the solution" reflects Catholic theology that calls each person to stand in solidarity with the suffering and marginalized peoples of the world by taking action to change their situation. Students are invited to contribute to building the kingdom of God through personal responsibility and constructive action. This messaging is inserted into "campaigns" around specific issues that the church has prioritized, including climate change, the plight of migrants, human trafficking, and global hunger. Student ambassadors respond to these issues through prayer, education, and action on their campuses, and together the campus chapters form a national movement to promote change.

CRS Student Ambassador Chapters
as Small Christian Communities

Pope Francis describes small Christian communities (SCCs) as "a source of enrichment for the Church, raised up by the Spirit for evangelizing different areas and sectors" (*Evangelii Gaudium*, no. 29). The "area" of the CRS student ambassador chapters is college campuses in the United States, and their "sector" is Catholic social teaching.

SCCs take a variety of forms but have common characteristics, which are described in part in three core papal encyclicals on Catholic mission: *Evangelii Nuntiandi,* written by Pope Paul VI in 1975; *Redemptoris Missio*, written by Pope John Paul II in 1990; and *Evangelii Gaudium*, written by Pope Francis in 2013. SCCs are an important way for ordinary Christians, including young Catholics on campus, to live out their Catholic identity and contribute meaningfully to the mission of the church. Emerging from these documents are four identifiable characteristics of SCCs that align with the experience, work, and identity of CRS student ambassador groups across the United States today: content, ecclesiology, participation, and mission.

Content

These are groups of Christians who . . . come together for prayer, Scripture reading, catechesis and discussion on human and ecological problems with a view to a common commitment. (*Redemptoris Missio*, no. 51)

There are many types of groups that gather intentionally around a particular type of content—a knitting club, book club, college alumni chapter. SCCs come together in a way that draws attention to a particular kind of content: prayer, scripture, Catholic teaching, and reflection on the "signs of the times" (*Evangelii Gaudium,* no. 51).

Picture yourself on a Sunday night, after the 6:00 p.m. mass and dinner. You make your way over to the CRS student ambassador meeting to join fellow students who are getting ready to share in an opening prayer, provided by CRS, on the current migration crisis, and then to reflect on how the readings and homily at mass reminded us of our baptismal call to create a more just world and especially to "welcome the stranger" among us. As the meeting continues, the president of the CRS student ambassador group shares a new resource received in a recent email from CRS staff, a "Catholic Social Teaching 101" video on the dignity of work, highlighting church teaching on how workers should be treated. This provides a quick catechetical lesson, tracing back to scripture and formally articulated by Pope

Leo XIII in his 1891 encyclical *Rerum Novarum*. This leads to conversation and questions—why are workers' rights still an issue today? How are our lives involved? How does it relate to the current migration crisis?

Another group leader mentions that the people who grow the coffee beans for our morning latte, who harvest cotton for our cheap-as-possible screen-printed T's for the homecoming football game, and who mine the minerals and metals found in our phones, tablets, and laptops are often trafficked, underpaid, and exploited. Someone takes out a phone to search the CRS website and finds examples of the agency's work with farming communities in Burkina Faso and mining communities in Peru. The ambassadors agree that they want to share these stories with others, to advocate to Congress for greater supply-chain transparency, and to commit to drinking ethically sourced coffee as much as possible—so, with guidance provided by CRS, they design a plan of action for their campus. This is the content of an SCC, the content that CRS student ambassadors grapple with, and the motivating reason for them to gather and then to take action.

Villanova University, Philadelphia

Villanova University has pioneered a now national model of integrating prayer, scripture, education, and action into one campus-wide event. At Villanova, the "Interfaith Solidarity Vigil for Refugees, Migrants and Victims of Human Trafficking" can fill a church on a Tuesday night. The event gathers the community together to reflect and act for the common good. In this way the CRS student ambassador community extends to the larger campus because of its creative, compelling, and integrated content.

Ecclesiology

[SCCs exist] within the Church, having solidarity with her life, being nourished by her teaching and united with her pastors. . . . They remain firmly attached to the local Church in which they are inserted, and to the universal Church, thus avoiding the very real danger of becoming isolated within themselves." (*Evangelii Nuntiandi*, no. 58)

It is not by accident that CRS student ambassadors are formally located and supported within a campus structure in a way that is part of the institutional Catholic Church. Their "home" is either a Catholic campus or a Newman Center, which may also be part of a local Catholic parish. Because of this catholicity, CRS student ambassadors are welcoming of all students of goodwill who identify with the mission of embodying Catholic social teaching.

In a country and world where young people are statistically leaving the Catholic Church at alarming rates, often during their college years, the CRS student ambassador program is providing an SCC experience for thousands of young people, helping them to stay connected to their Catholic faith and identity. In 2016–17 there were over eight hundred trained CRS student ambassador leaders, reaching more than forty thousand college students. Describing the experience, one ambassador articulated: "The CRS student ambassador program is wonderful because of its connection right back to the church and the service of the most vulnerable. It is amazing that at our seemingly insular campuses, we have the potential to join the greater body of Christ through solidarity and compassion."

Kent State University: University Parish Newman Center, Kent, Ohio

Many of our student chapters, including Kent State University, are Newman Centers that are connected with local parishes. This provides rich opportunity for collaboration beyond just a campus club. Kent State University CRS student ambassadors, for example, hold CRS ethical-trade sales in conjunction with parishioners and thus have the chance to interact with the wider Catholic Church, even during their time as college students.

Participation

He or she is playing an active role and is encouraged to share in the common task. (*Redemptoris Missio*, no. 51)

CRS student ambassadors are connected to their ambassador community and empowered to participate actively, which then thrusts them into authentic communion with other CRS student ambassadors, the mission of CRS, and the lives of our brothers and sisters around the world. One staff advisor of CRS student ambassadors reflects: "CRS treats our students like adults and empowers them to truly share in the mission of the organization. I have never seen students make a commitment like they have with CRS ambassadors."

Participation goes beyond the internal community within the CRS student ambassador group and expands to a notion of participation in a larger community—national, international, spiritual. CRS brings the chapter leaders and staff together every other year for a national conference in order to sustain a sense of national movement, and through regular communication keeps them in touch with one another and the work of CRS overseas. The hope is that this deep experience of being empowered, formed as leaders, and convicted in their call to "boldly take the initiative" (*Evangelii Gaudium*, no. 54) shapes the way they will continue to live their lives, participating in church and society.

Ohio State University: Saint Thomas More Newman Center, Columbus

For Mary Chudy, peer minister for social concerns and co-leader of the CRS student ambassador chapter, a clear example of authentic participation is the way in which students are able to focus on accomplishing tasks, such as planning for student events, in a meaningful way. She is struck by their ability to find balance between getting lost in deep conversation and also getting the details planned, all while taking seriously the contributions of each individual toward the larger efforts. She was amazed at "how quickly the hours of planning passed by" in the context of their community.

Mission

[SCCs] become a leaven of Christian life, of care for the poor and neglected, and of commitment to the transformation of society. (*Redemptoris Missio*, no. 51)

SCCs are mission oriented, and mission is at the heart of the CRS student ambassador movement. One CRS student ambassador articulated this well: "The best part of the CRS student ambassador program is the feeling that you're actually making a difference on campus. . . . With CRS, we're actively putting forth effort to make positive change in the world around us." The mantra, "I am the cause. I am the solution," grounds students in reflection on the church's social mission, shared responsibility for human suffering, and concrete action that makes a difference.

If we put ourselves back in the CRS student ambassador meeting after the 6:00 p.m. Sunday mass, we might find ourselves being strategic about our response to worker exploitation. Because we are mission oriented, we are active. We all pull out our phones and sign the CRS "I Am Human Trafficking" letter about supply-chain transparency and plan a day when we can set up a table in the campus quad to invite the rest of our community to sign the same letter, highlighting our conviction that people and planet matter just as much as profit. We might lead a campaign to have our bookstore carry fair-trade clothing, which includes educating ourselves on the issue, reaching out to collaborate with other groups on campus, and dialoguing with campus administration. We might plan a holiday fair-trade sale to ensure that our community has access to ethically produced gifts for Christmas. No matter which campus we are on, we pray, learn, reflect, and then take action to transform ourselves, our campus, and the world.

University of the Incarnate Word, San Antonio, Texas

CRS student ambassadors at the University of the Incarnate Word care about the issue of human trafficking, which led them to host an opportunity for the larger campus community to get involved and make a difference. They shared global and local stories of how the issue affects people during an "I Am Human Trafficking Solidarity Walk" and also invited people to sign advocacy letters oriented toward affecting policy change. Additionally, they raffled off some fair-trade items, while sharing the importance of purchasing ethically in order to ensure that students are not unintentionally contributing to slave labor.

Challenges

Busy Schedules

CRS student ambassadors identify their schedules as their biggest challenge—their busy lives are filled with classes, other leadership positions, socializing, volunteering, and (sometimes!) even sleeping, all of which are in direct competition with their ability to dedicate as much time and energy as they would like to their passion for making a difference in their communities and in the world. The full schedules of students, as well as plentiful lists of student clubs on each campus, present a related challenge: sometimes student ambassador chapters struggle to grow their communities. CRS seeks to help students approach this challenge creatively, by seeing their commitment to peace and justice as something that can be integrated seamlessly into the rest of their lives, not as something that needs to stand separately as one among many competing priorities.

Complex Issues

The work and mission of CRS globally is complex, and there are no easy solutions. This is challenging for CRS student ambassador communities who want to make a difference. Additionally, the issues are complex in their intersection with events and policies in the church and society. Sometimes CRS student ambassadors find important topics difficult to discuss based on increasingly polarized viewpoints within the US context due to contention around a Catholic perspective on migration, climate change, and international aid. CRS seeks to help students live in the tension of these complexities, both by helping them to understand the issues more deeply through encountering the stories of real people around the world, and by discerning how the wisdom of Catholic social teaching invites us to respond.

Conclusion: After Graduation

The experience of CRS student ambassadors does not end with graduation. Students articulate that, for them, CRS involvement is a "conviction, not a club," and convictions last well beyond four years of higher education. Their SCC formation in lifelong values will continue to unfold for each and every individual. In this way the hope and dream is that CRS student ambassadors will bring these convictions to bear for the rest of their lives—in their future communities, workplaces, families, parishes, and decisions of all kinds, seeking in every moment to recognize their role in the "cause" of complex issues and their potential to be part of the "solution" as we work to make the kingdom of God more fully present across the globe.

10

Small Group Journey in Discipleship

Duke Catholic Center

MICHAEL T. MARTIN, OFM CONV

The Duke Catholic Center is the Catholic campus ministry of Duke University in Durham, North Carolina. The university's student body comprises sixty-five hundred undergraduate and seventy-five hundred graduate or professional students; Catholics make up approximately 20 percent of the student body (twenty-eight hundred students). Roman Catholicism is the largest single denomination on campus. Although a college in the Quaker and Methodist traditions for regional southeastern students in the 1800s, the university has grown to welcome an international student body that is ranked in the top ten of the country annually. Students who attend Duke University are in the highest percentile academically and come from a wide range of socioeconomic backgrounds. With a relatively high tuition, the students who make up a simple majority of the student body usually come from families of means.

Catholic campus ministry has had a small presence from its inception in the early twentieth century, but the first records of organized campus ministry are not noted until 1934. A priest from the local parish was assigned to serve the student body on a part-time basis until 1974, when the first full-time chaplain was assigned. As the Catholic population grew, so too did the ministry and the staffing.

The Catholic presence grew even more substantially with the appointment of Fr. Joseph Vetter as campus ministry director in 1998. As a priest of the Diocese of Raleigh, he was able to promote Catholic life on campus in a more mainstream way, and he heightened the visibility of the programming by augmenting the small office space in the basement of Duke Chapel with the purchase of a house to serve as a locus for Catholic life across the street from the campus.

While some forms of small groups had existed at the center for a number of years as Bible study groups, it was in the early 2000s that they became a more active part of the campus ministry. The emergence of the "Awakening" retreat program (developed by the Catholic campus ministry at Texas A&M) deepened the spiritual life of students. This program also contained a follow-up component called "Fourth Day," a weekly small group for retreat participants.

Through 2010, the majority of the small group experience on campus was a Bible study model. Usually, the group began with "Highs and Lows"—students would take turns describing a really good thing and a really bad thing that happened in the last week. The group leader would then read prepared information regarding a specific scripture passage that the group would reflect upon together. The group would conclude with intercessory prayer. Sometimes the scripture that was used for reflection was the coming or previous Sunday's gospel; other times a certain book or letter was examined from start to finish. Usually there were seven to eight students in a group. The combined groups averaged about forty students weekly, almost all of whom were undergraduates.

In July 2010, the leadership of the Duke Catholic Center was given to the Conventual Franciscan Friars, and I was assigned to be the director. During my first year I simply observed the existing model and tried to ascertain from students the level of impact and the possibilities for growth. A few realities emerged:

- These groups were not evangelical, and they were more supportive of students who were members. While important and powerful for those students, the groups were viewed by most others as cliquish and for the "really holy."
- It was difficult to get student leaders for the small groups because the leadership responsibility was seen as almost akin to teaching a class in terms of preparation. The student leaders felt it was imperative to know as much as possible about the passage in order to lead a discussion about it. With that daunting task, recruiting leaders was challenging.
- The "Highs and Lows" section of the group experience was becoming almost half (if not more) of the meeting time. While seen as helpful, it tended to miss the mark for the small group experience's real purpose: growing closer to Christ through the scriptures.

I was confident that with some adjustments to the model, we could see substantive change in the quality of the small groups and in the fruits they would bring forth in our community. For the next two years I tried to supervise some changes, particularly around structure of the small group meeting experience as well as resources to facilitate discussion and growth. All of our groups began reflecting on the coming Sunday's gospel, with good resources in hand and directives for how to engage in a group reflection on scripture. That seemed to me to be a sufficient recipe for quality small group engagement. How wrong I was!

I am not too proud to admit that I wasted two years on this process, not believing that I (we) needed help. I failed to appreciate a number of dynamics that are essential to healthy small group ministry on a college campus; more important, I failed to realize that there were some people out there who were truly gifted and skilled in assisting in this process on college campuses. I had heard of a number of them before (FOCUS, The Evangelical Catholic, St. Paul's Outreach, among others), but I thought they were more for campus ministries that didn't have their act together or for campuses that had very little staffing.

The Evangelical Catholic had been ministering in our diocese for a number of years, and I had gotten to know their director, Jason Simon. After some conversation we decided to engage its services and signed a three-year alliance. This was a game changer and has made a huge difference in this area of our ministry. One of the reasons I believed Evangelical Catholic was the best fit for our campus was its emphasis on training our students to be leaders. We did not have any of Evangelical Catholic's personnel come on to our campus to run small groups—rather, with Evangelical Catholic's help, we began to train our own students to lead our small groups. That was a decision that has reaped benefits that we are still unpacking.

Small Communities at Duke Today

Our current small group ministry is an active and evangelical dimension of our campus ministry. While not all students participate, all students are aware that we believe this to be the primary way in which we can reach more and more Catholic students on our campus. Certainly, the Eucharist is the "source and summit" of all that we do. However, getting disengaged Catholics to reawaken the gift of faith in their lives during the college years will probably not be accomplished by simply inviting them to mass. Instead, peers inviting peers to small group meetings that take place in dorms and other spots around campus to hear one another reflect on the work of the Holy Spirit in their lives—that can and does rekindle the flame of faith that leads students back to the Eucharist. That is a primary goal of our campus ministry, and all other nonliturgical programming is subordinate to it.

The Duke Catholic Center currently has nine full-time staff members, with six in frontline ministry and three in support roles. Of the six, one currently coordinates the small group ministry, among a number of other ministerial responsibilities. In the summer of 2018, that person will become our full-time director of small group ministry as we will be adding two additional full-time staff members. The remaining five ministers work with the current coordinator in visioning as well as carrying out the specifics of the ministry. Most of the staff work at this time is spent in leadership training, one-on-one ministry, and material support creation.

While we initially used the materials provided by Evangelical Catholic, we have grown to develop some of our own under Evangelical Catholic's supervision. We publish a leader's booklet each semester that includes an outline and discussion suggestions to serve as a guide. We use Evangelical Catholic's materials for the training of our student leaders to help them to appreciate the bigger picture of what we are doing, as well as to show how their growth in faith affects their own and others' lives.

We have used some of Evangelical Catholic's training camps, but found that logistics with our students warranted a more tailored program that fits student schedules. As a result, we now run our own training program that we have titled Duc in Altum (Latin for "put out into the deep"). This name suggests the stretch that we are challenging our student leaders to embrace. These four-day/three-night intensive retreat and training experiences are currently held during the first days of January before classes begin and during the fall break in October. We began with only undergraduates, but we now have undergraduates and graduate or professional students participating together in these training experiences. Also, we now have students leading major portions of the training. These training retreats are followed by one-on-one meetings that six staff members carry out with small group leaders on a bi-weekly basis.

Recruitment for small groups takes place at two times: at the beginning of the semester, and by invitation of members or expressed interest by a student at any time. At Duke, we have small groups that meet during the fall and spring semesters, as well as during the summer sessions on campus. At the beginning of each semester two students (one undergraduate and one graduate) give a brief witness talk at the end of Sunday masses, with sign-up cards at every seat. Students fill them out, and that night and the next night leaders make phone calls to get those who expressed interest slotted into a group time that fits their schedule. There are groups that meet on all different nights in different locations at different times, so almost everyone's schedule can be accommodated.

A typical small group at Duke has approximately ten to fifteen members. This is too large, but as we are still young in this ministry (four years), we do not as yet have as many trained leaders as we need. We project that in another two years that issue should be minimized with the leaders that we currently have in training. Usually, leaders are asked to put in an hour during the week in prayer and preparation for the specific meeting. They open with some spontaneous prayer and usually have a warm-up discussion that is related to the theme of the gospel for the coming Sunday. Then a member is asked to read aloud the gospel, and all sit in silence afterward, pondering specifics of the text that come to mind. Another member is asked to read the gospel aloud a second time, with silence to follow again. Discussion then follows with three types of questions: observation, understanding, and application. The meeting generally concludes with intercessory prayer. Small group leaders are encouraged to check in with group members at least bi-weekly to discuss their own faith journey in the church.

The challenges that we continue to face in small group ministry are probably similar to most other campuses. It is an issue getting students to appreciate that this can and will be a lifelong experience that can affect their spiritual lives as well as the lives of their faith communities. Helping students to see that they don't need to be faultless to engage in this ministry is a challenge. Encouraging students to make the time for training can be difficult when so many other voices are calling for their time. The challenges are in no way insurmountable, however—they are overshadowed by the graces of the ministry.

Impact

We have been overwhelmed by the depth of spirituality that can emerge on the part of leaders and members alike. This ministry has allowed so many students to see the call to discipleship in Christ and then to accept the Great Commission as the mandate from Jesus to us all. We struggle with the "how" of this ministry more than anything else—how to reach the most? But allow this testimonial from one of our student leaders used in an end-of-mass recruitment message to speak for itself:

> Small faith sharing groups have transformed my relationship with Christ. A year ago, I would have described Jesus simply as a safety net. With every mistake and in every failure, Jesus was my source of strength and resilience. I was able to carry on with my life. But I was consistently left longing for more. Maybe you've felt that way too.
>
> However, Jesus as a "safety net" or "book on a shelf—to be used at our whim and need" is not good enough. He invites us to more. The Lord wants to be our best friend. This is the ideal we are striving for.
>
> Some of you may be thinking, "I don't need that. I am comfortable with where I am right now in my faith life." But as a people of God we are called to comfort the disturbed, and to disturb the comfortable. Small group will provide a forum to do just that.
>
> Others of you may feel you have a good prayer life and routine set. That's great! But we are ceaselessly called to dig deeper into the person of Christ in prayer, and specifically through the scriptures. We are challenged to strive for holiness in what Matthew Kelly calls "becoming a better version of you." There's still more work left to do.
>
> And for those of you who feel completely lost, Jesus is reaching out his hand to you as well in the form of this

community and this opportunity. Trust in him, and trust in the faith, fortitude, and witness of your peers.

Here is your invitation. This is your opportunity. Growth, inspiration, happiness, community, peace, challenge, and trust are all potential results of joining a small group. We want you to meet our best friend. We want you to rediscover the person of Jesus Christ. We are opening this door for you today. Don't be afraid. Take the next steps. He is patiently waiting to unfurl the richness of his love in your life.

11

Leadership Labs

Small Groups at the University of Hawai'i

CHRISTOPHER DERIGE MALANO

Campus ministry can be a moment in a collegian's life that is filled with events or it can be a time when potential is unleashed. Students are often asked to take on responsibility in the church, but due to lack of proper formation and sound theological grounding, or even the availability of time, they end up as convenient poster children of youth and young adult engagement. It is often heard that the young are the leaders of tomorrow, but tomorrow is already here, and it is already too late to realize that prior generations had set them up for failure.

In a professional field where outputs can be more important than outcomes and where data drives ministry, students themselves might be introduced to the equation far too late in the process, or even worse, too easily left out. This field that is constantly haunted by diminishing financial resources can be tempted by focusing its mission toward maintaining a certain appeal to donors or drowned in the sea of grant writing and reporting. This is a reality for many campus ministries, and perhaps it is no surprise that the overwhelming majority of institutions of higher education do not have a pastoral presence.

A new, yet not so new, model of reaching out to students ought to be rediscovered. With the difficulty of maintaining professional pastoral staff on campuses, there needs to be a shift toward empowering students themselves to be the primary agents in campus ministry. This was the case at the advent of the university apostolate and can perhaps be an insight for preparing the current and future generations of student leaders in the church. Coupled with the fact that a new generation of students (Generation Z or iGeneration) is entering higher education, it is imperative that campus ministries take the lead in aligning the church to the realities of the twenty-first century.

Marked by recent institutional change and amid several challenges, the Newman Center at the University of Hawaiʻi–Mānoa, has turned itself into a laboratory for testing new models of student leadership in campus ministry.

Campus Ministry in Hawaiʻi

There has been a Catholic presence at the University of Hawaiʻi for nearly seventy years. Before it was a university parish, the Newman Center started off in the 1950s as the Newman Apostolate. The pastoral presence of the church at the university was due to the initiative and energy of Fr. Dan Dever, who gathered students regularly for liturgy and began to build a community. In 1982, the Society of Jesus (Jesuits) and the Sisters of Saint Francis collaborated with the Diocese of Honolulu to build a Newman Center adjacent to the university. The Newman Center was eventually recognized as a diocesan parish with a twofold mission: to minister to the young adults as a Catholic campus ministry, and to serve the diverse population of island residents.

In the 1990s the Newman Center, with the operational support of the Diocese of Honolulu, became the hub for campus ministry throughout the state of Hawaiʻi. Its pastor also served as the diocesan director for campus ministry. This allowed for an expansion of the number of campus ministers, who would be tasked with outreach to the other campuses throughout the Hawaiian archipelago, including community colleges.

The Jesuits decided to leave the Hawaiian Islands in 2011, and the Diocese of Honolulu resumed the responsibility of the Newman Center–Holy Spirit Parish and its campus ministry to the University of Hawaiʻi–Mānoa. By this time funding for this coordinated model of organizing campus ministry in the state dried up, and the intentional diocesan-wide outreach was significantly reduced. There was virtually no other presence of the church in the other state university or community-college campuses.

The current pastoral team at the Newman Center comprises a full-time diocesan priest, who is the pastor and director of campus ministry; a full-time lay pastoral administrator; and a part-time lay campus minister. In order to accomplish all that is necessary for the operations of a parish, there is a need for more staff. However, with budgetary constraints, hiring additional staff is not possible. From this bleak situation emerged an opportunity to rethink how to continue the functioning of the parish while not compromising the coordination of campus ministry activities.

A Diverse Student Body

Mānoa is the flagship campus of the University of Hawaiʻi system. There are about 17,600 enrolled students, about 13,000 of whom are undergraduate students; 66 percent of the students are from the state of Hawaiʻi, 28 percent from out of state, and 6 percent are international students. No one ethnicity is a majority, though Asian students are the largest block at 36 percent.[1] While there are no statistics available about the religious make-up of the student body, it is estimated that there are about three thousand Catholic

---

[1] "About UH Mānoa," University of Hawaiʻi–Mānoa, www.manoa.hawaii. edu.

students attending the Mānoa campus. However, only about three hundred students are on the email distribution list.

The students participating in campus ministry and the registered Newman Club are as diverse as the demographics of the university. Students from the state of Hawai'i are from every island; a large percentage of mainland students are from California; and others are from the East Coast. As the East West Center, a program of the US federal government, is just a few minutes' walk from the Newman Center, there is a robust number of international students, with all continents represented. This reality posed several challenges in terms of outreach approach and also provided an equal amount of opportunity in building bridges within the student population.

Building Student Leadership

Limited financial resources have provided the Newman Center with the opportunity to rethink the role of students in campus ministry. Previous models of organizing students placed the campus ministers as the central producers of programming, while the students were consumers of programming; in other words, ministry was done for and not *by* the students. In recent years a shift has taken place, and students have become the driving force of campus ministry. This did not happen overnight, and it remains a work in progress.

Leadership Vacuum

The Newman Center receives students who have had varied experiences in the church, but only a few have had previous leadership experience, for example, as youth ministry animators or as catechists in their home parishes. Those who possess some leadership skills are often already overcommitted in multiple academic or student groups on campus or in ministries at their home parishes.

There is also a "brain drain" of sorts, as many students with the greatest involvement in the church and the most formation in leadership skills seek to study outside Hawai'i.

Given the small number of students who have had previous ministry experience, coupled with a limited number of pastoral staff, student recruitment becomes a twofold effort: first, reaching out as widely as possible to the student body as a whole to inform students of the services provided by the Newman Center, inviting them to events and liturgies; and second, keeping an eye out for students who have the potential to serve as student leaders.

Leadership Development

To tackle the question of capacity building, the pastoral staff developed a leadership training camp prior to the start of the academic year focusing on the skills necessary for peer-to-peer ministry. Topics of the camp included getting-to-know-you activities, team building, understanding their role as leaders from a theological perspective, communication, visioning, and project-management training. Some critiques of the students were that they already knew the topics discussed, partly because they had learned about them in their studies or they knew from their experience in previous years in leadership. The weekend camp was ultimately curtailed due to a threat of a hurricane hitting Oahu.

To allow more freedom for students to envision and develop their programs, they were expected to use an online project-management tool that would help them with time management and identify the kinds and number of volunteers they would need and when. This also provided the campus minister with a method to monitor progress, as well as spot potential problems in advance, without an overbearing presence or sense of nagging. At the end of the year it was evident that what the students claimed to already know in theory did not necessarily transfer to practice. This only reinforces the need for leadership formation programs, throughout the year if possible.

Student leaders expressed a wish for greater autonomy in their programs. However, it was a great risk and required trust on the part of the pastoral staff that the students would follow through with the programs to which they were committed. While the previous year the critique was that the student leaders were simply implementing programs that someone else had developed, the student leaders' critiques the following year included that the project management tool made them feel micromanaged. The implementation of that tool, though it did promote transparency, was perhaps seen as a means for uncharitable rebuking. The questions to be explored are how much independence should be given to student leaders, and at what point professional staff should intervene (and to what degree).

The change from having students implement programs to having students be the generators and developers of programs was a major shift in how campus ministry was done at the Newman Center. It was perhaps too much, too fast. A more metered scaffolding of introducing new leadership themes with each successive year might help to manage the push back from the students, who may not necessarily see in that moment the bigger picture of what is trying to be achieved—a culture shift in student leadership in campus ministry. More important than developing the skills of a new generation of leaders in the church is guiding the students to understand that their leadership role is not as simple as being a machine that produces programs and events for the sake of having to do so, but to realize that their leadership is a vocation originating from their baptism.

Organizing in Small Groups

Wednesday Night Mass

The main small group gathering that exists as part of the campus ministry occurs during the weekly Wednesday night candlelight mass at 9:00 p.m. After a brief homily by the presiding priest, a student gives a brief reflection or testimony and then poses a question to the group for discussion. Students split up and organize themselves in small groups of three or four. Unlike other campus ministries where small groups have a fixed enrollment, the small groups at the candlelight mass were self-elected based upon the attendance of that particular week. This method of small groups was developed by the Student Council because the general attendance was small enough to ensure that every person would eventually meet. The concern of the pastoral staff was that students would eventually settle into their usual seats and, being comfortable with where they were seated, they would tend to sit with the same people or naturally gravitate to their peers for discussion groups. A gentle reminder to the student coordinator would be made occasionally with the suggestion of changing up the process of regrouping students. As with student leadership skills, there is a gap between the ideal and actual practice. Again, the question for consideration is how much intervention on behalf of the pastoral staff is necessary to maintain a sense of independence and trust that the student leaders are aware of the inadvertent formation of cliques.

Laudato Si' *Groups*

The model of having small groups that would meet on a regular basis throughout the semester was discussed with the student leaders. It was determined that there was, for the moment, little interest in leading something with what was perceived as an immense commitment. Meanwhile, their fellow students asked about small groups—usually with an expectation that someone else would coordinate it and they would simply participate. The culture of maximizing benefit with minimal commitment needed to be explored because the dominating concern was the amount of time that would be needed to fulfill the commitment.

The different liturgical seasons provided an opportunity for the student leaders to explore the possibility of shorter commitments in leading small groups. One such opportunity came about in the spring of 2016: to engage in Pope Francis's encyclical *Laudato Si'* during the lenten season. Exploration of the themes of the encyclical in small student groups emerged out of a parish-wide reading group that took place the prior semester. While the parish discussion took on more of an informational tone, the students were looking for an approach that asked, "How does this affect me?"

The student coordinator for the Wednesday night candlelight mass was responsible for recruiting six students who would focus on the theme for one week. This allowed the student leader not to feel overwhelmed by having to prepare six sessions, and in turn, it presented the opportunity for six other students to participate in a specific and short one-off commitment. "Lent 4.2," a resource developed by Passionist priest Fr. Joseph Mitchell, CP, was used as a starting point for the students and helped to guide the small group discussions during the season of Lent.[2] Each week had a general theme:

Ash Wednesday—Christian simplicity
Week 1—food
Week 2—consumption
Week 3—water
Week 4—energy
Week 5—transportation
Holy Week—gratitude and generosity

Each weekly handout contained points of information, quotations from the encyclical or other Catholic social teaching, and steps for personal action. The student responsible for giving the reflection was tasked with the goal of trying to connect the gospel of the day with the theme of the week. The connection was not always evident for the student or the coordinator and often needed greater participation of the pastoral staff to discuss and illustrate the relationships that might be made.

---

[2] Joseph Mitchell, CP, "Lent 4.2," www.lent42.org.

Small Groups, Big Impacts

There were several significant results that came about through these small group discussions. Though the number of participants was relatively small, their recommendations were well received by the parish at large. The initial actions naturally resulted in subsequent ones. Here are some of the parish-wide actions and suggestions that resulted:

- Purchasing paper plates and cold and hot cups rather than plastic or Styrofoam, even though it costs more.
- Using biodegradable coffee stirrers rather than plastic.
- Whenever possible, using reusable dishes rather than disposable ones.
- Coordinating with the university to increase recycling efforts of metals, glass, plastics, paper, and cardboard.
- Purchasing recycled paper, even though it costs more.
- Installing a smart-watering system that does not turn on when there has been rainfall.
- Replacing incandescent and fluorescent light bulbs with LED lights.
- Purchasing a locally grown pine tree for Christmas rather than a "traditional" tree that is shipped from the mainland.
- Installing photovoltaic solar panels to reduce the center's dependency on energy generated from petroleum and coal.

The true measure of the success of this exercise was not the fact that there was a resource to use in guiding the discussion, but in realizing that it was simply a starting point. The unforeseen benefit of accompanying the students (the ones who offered the reflection and the coordinator) was the opportunity to help them to realize that they were not bound to the text on the weekly handouts. Once they were exposed to the opportunities that came about because of this, they also quickly grasped that it would require additional time and effort to adapt the resource to better fit their voice and more effectively address their concerns. At this point, when students are tempted to choose the easier route, it was the role of the pastoral staff to speak about what it was that they really wanted to accomplish—just to "get it over with" or a potentially transformational moment. The difficulty for the campus minister is to accept and be at peace with the possibility of the student choosing the less desired route.

In addition to the practical changes that were adopted by the parish, there were several interesting observations made as part of the lenten small group sharing. It is no secret that the state of Hawai'i is completely surrounded by the vast Pacific Ocean. The threats of hurricanes and tsunamis happen on a yearly basis. In case of an emergency it would take at least one week before any significant amount of supplies would arrive from the continental United States, the nearest landmass. It was not surprising to hear the amount of anxiety that arose when discussing the vulnerability of the state should it be affected by a natural disaster. The student leaders were adept at shifting the tone from one of despair and helplessness to one of empowerment and action. Students were invited to explore how small personal decisions could have an impact on a national or global scale. Using additional resources provided by Catholic Relief Services, such as the *Laudato Si'* edition of *Community Reflections*, helped to facilitate subsequent discussions.[3]

A Generation of Empowered Leadership

In a hyper-globalized age it is often too easy to use resources that have already been prepared, which also saves time. They are a good starting point, but effective programming should respond to the actual needs and concerns of the students, not to their perceived needs. Not taking the time to engage and accompany

---

[3] *2016 Community Reflections: Laudato Si' Edition* (Baltimore: Catholic Relief Services, 2015).

students, however, in some sense does a disservice to the church in that it does not prepare leaders to fully engage in their apostolate in a way that empowers them to develop and advance ministry. Simply having students implement programs is a quick fix—programs are executed, checklists are completed—but it does not address the deeper concern of an underdeveloped youth leadership in the church. It is a question that perhaps Pope Francis is hoping to address in the upcoming Synod of Bishops on young people, the faith, and vocational discernment.

Guiding students to understand the needs of their peers, analyze socially, reflect theologically, and create programs that are meaningful to their time and space is a slow and arduous process. It requires much time to be present, listen, and foster a relationship of interdependence. Slow as it may be, it is a holistic path that truly empowers students in name and in practice. It requires constant dialogue with students, willingness to relinquish power and privilege, an immense amount of humility, courage to seek reconciliation often, and above all, trust in God.

12

From Parishes to Small Groups

Evolving Models at the Newman Catholic Center of Sacramento

CECILIA FLORES

The Newman Catholic Center Sacramento is one of three Newman Centers that are run by the Diocese of Sacramento, California. The centers had previously functioned as parishes, with campus ministry being just one of the many ministries offered. In 2013, Bishop Jaime Soto, concerned about the number of young adults, particularly university students, leaving the faith, made a decision to transition the permanent communities that had formed at the centers to neighboring parishes and to revamp each center to focus solely on ministry to college students. Under the parish model, outreach to college students was limited, often lost in the shuffle with the competing needs of community members from all life stages.

The transition started at the center in Davis, California, followed by Chico, California, and in 2015 the transition process began at the center in Sacramento. The Sacramento center is now in its second full academic year functioning solely as a base for campus ministry in the greater Sacramento area.

Part of the vision in the change of model was to also reach out to college-aged students attending community colleges or other university campuses in the areas surrounding the center. For the center in Sacramento that includes its main feeder campus, California State University, Sacramento (CSUS), as well as five major community colleges, one large Christian university (William Jessup), and numerous vocational schools.

Building Student Leaders

Each Newman Center has two full-time paid staff members: a director and an hourly campus minister. Notably missing from the staff is a priest-chaplain; however, the center has a number of priests from neighboring parishes who commit a significant amount of their time to help with the sacramental and pastoral needs of the students.

The paid staff is complemented and enhanced by the Student Leadership Council, which is composed of volunteering students and young alumni who dedicate their time to serving the Newman community in a variety of different functions. The council is headed by an executive board, which consists of a president, vice president, secretary, treasurer, and outreach coordinator.

Each large ministry is run by a committee, led by the committee chair and co-chairs. Ministries that fall under this structure are ones that require a significant amount of preparation and coordination and include liturgy, music, retreat, facility management, outreach, and Newman nights, which are weekly evening socials.

In addition to the large ministries, there are a number of small faith sharing groups, each with a specific focus and target audience. Each small faith sharing group is led by a facilitator and co-facilitator when applicable.

With the limited number of staff, programming depends heavily on the work of the student leaders. When more students are willing to lead, more programs are able to be offered, thus expanding the opportunities for outreach to the student community.

Since the Newman Catholic Center Sacramento does not have any official affiliation with CSUS, our student leaders also concurrently run the Newman Catholic Club at the university, which is an officially recognized student organization. Student leaders who attend CSUS are appointed club officers, and the club status enables the campus ministry to be present on the campus itself for monthly meetings, tabling, and holding special events.

The Student Leadership Council started off with thirteen members at the beginning of the fall 2016 semester and has grown to twenty-eight members entering spring 2018. Most leaders attend CSUS; however, there are a number of leaders who attend other institutions in the area.

Various recruitment methods are employed in order to attract new leaders. Applications are accepted twice a year, at the end of the fall and spring semesters. Announcements are made at student masses, and a call for applications is blasted throughout social media. The most effective method, however, has been personal invitations, as potential leaders are identified by staff or current leaders.

Community of Communities

The faith-sharing groups are considered to be a community of communities—meaning that the Newman community, though one, comprises numerous smaller groups, each contributing something unique to the whole. Each small faith-sharing group is born of a need and/or common interest that is identified by the students themselves. Most groups meet weekly, although a few meet bi-weekly or seasonally. The groups that we currently have cover a wide range of topics and interests.

There is a men's group and a women's group, which are gender specific and discuss topics related to masculinity and femininity in a Catholic perspective. There is also a Lectio Divina group that meets weekly on campus for those who enjoy prayer with the scriptures. Another group meets weekly on campus to pray the Rosary. There are also groups specific to age, such as our alumni group, which focuses on those who have recently graduated, and our dorm group that caters toward the freshmen and sophomores living on campus.

With the ever-increasing ethnic diversity in the greater Sacramento area, a number of small groups have been formed to reach out to specific cultural communities. There are currently two Filipino-based movements that operate within the Newman structure: Couples for Christ USA, and Foundation for Family and Life. These movements run their campus ministry programs through our center, and numerous young Filipinos who grew up in either of these movements have quickly integrated into the Newman Center by means of the small groups that they each run. There is also a Pastoral Universitaria faith-sharing group, whose purpose is to create a space for those who prefer to express their faith in Spanish or within Latino Catholic culture.

Each group uses a method that best works for the needs of its small group. Some choose to have frequent structured prayer, while others focus more on building community through social activity. What is common to all groups, however, is the open dialogue that exists among members. Facilitators are encouraged to be open to feedback and change, aware of each member's needs and expectations, and also to be understanding and supportive when people find what they are looking for in a different small group.

Challenges

One of the greatest challenges is the population the center is intended to serve. The main feeder campus, CSUS, is a commuter campus, with only 6 percent of the student population living on campus.[1] Additionally, over 50 percent are considered to be low income as defined by Federal Pell Grant Program eligibility requirements, and a recent report found that approximately thirty-six hundred CSUS students are homeless.[2]

---

[1] "California State University—Sacramento," *US News and World Report* (2017).

[2] Diana Lambert, "High Housing Prices Are Forcing Hundreds of Sacramento State Students into Homelessness," *The Sacramento Bee* (December 4, 2017).

· These facts prove challenging to a campus ministry program that depends greatly on students volunteering their time. The majority of students at CSUS and surrounding community colleges have to work, not to earn extra spending money but for survival. This means that they do not have as much free time to volunteer, even if they wish to do so. Also, many other students who still live and commute from home are already rooted and serving in their home parishes. These are a few factors that can limit the pool from which student leadership can be drawn.

To address this, the center takes an approach to leadership commitments that some may consider unconventional. Leaders are not required to contribute a minimum number of work hours or to be present at a certain number of trainings or meetings. They commit to serve in the ways they are able for the time that they can, and they are asked to be faithful and responsible to that commitment. Some leaders commit themselves to multiple ministries and spend a significant amount of time at the center, while others only commit to one ministry and are only present when that ministry meets. The culture of the Student Leadership Council is one of flexibility and understanding. Leaders are challenged not to compare their commitments to other leaders and are constantly reminded that faithfulness to one's commitment is what is expected, nothing more and nothing less. This culture is one that helps bring to life the idea of the church as the body of Christ, allowing the leaders to experience firsthand the need to appreciate and value each part of the body regardless of its size and functions in comparison to others.

Reflecting the Diversity of CSUS Students

The desire for the community to reflect the diversity of the region has also proven to be a challenge, not due to a lack of enthusiasm or desire to participate, but rather in resources that speak to the cultural religiosity of different groups. Campus ministry resources in the United States that are specific to Hispanic or Asian Pacific

Islander students are scarce to none, which is an alarming fact in light of recent data. According to a University of Notre Dame report, roughly 50 percent of Catholic teenagers no longer identify themselves as Catholic by the time they reach their late twenties.[3] Pew Research also reported that the Catholic populations of the United States have shifted from the Northeast and the Midwest to the West and the South, and that Catholics are more likely than any other set of Americans to be immigrants or children of immigrants, and also Hispanic.[4] An article in *Our Sunday Visitor* also reported that approximately 55 percent of all US Catholics under the age of thirty are Hispanic.[5] Additionally, Asians are now the fastest-growing racial group in the country.[6] Given these statistics, special attention and concern should be given to young Catholics, but even more specifically to young Catholics who are immigrants and/or children of immigrants.

Though it is true that the Catholic Church is universal, it cannot be denied that its lived expression, particularly for those who are immigrants or children of immigrants, comes in many different forms that are unknown or are not taken into consideration by the white religious hegemony in the United States. The majority of the resources and programs that exist for youth and young adults in the United States today are developed through an Anglo-American perspective and experience. Additionally, the great majority of speakers at national and regional conferences for the young Catholic population are white, which does not reflect the true diversity that exists in the young American church.

---

[3] Christian Smith and Nicolette Manglos-Weber, *Understanding Former Young Catholics: Findings from a National Study of American Emerging Adults* (Notre Dame, IN: University of Notre Dame, 2014).

[4] Michael Lipka, "A Closer Look at Catholic America," *Pew Research Center* blog (September 14, 2015).

[5] Hosffman Ospino, "The Church's Changing Face," *Our Sunday Visitor* (May 18, 2014).

[6] "The Rise of Asian Americans," *Pew Research Center's Social and Demographic Trends Project* blog (April 4, 2013).

For the Newman Center in Sacramento this has meant developing programs and methods of outreach that are new and unique. The desire to explore and define one's identity may be common to the adolescent and young adult experience, but this process is undoubtedly more complex for immigrants and/or children of immigrants, as they are often torn between different cultures, each with its own history, tradition, beliefs, and religious expression. The ethnic studies movement in universities has made great strides in addressing the identity crises experienced by young people of color. However, it is necessary to mention that this is oftentimes done independent of religion, or in a way that distances or alienates students from the religious beliefs of their parents. Because of this, campus ministry efforts at the Newman Center in Sacramento prioritize outreach to these groups, particularly the Hispanic populations, which together make up the most prominent group in the diocese. The goal is to create a space where people can freely discuss their own cultural and religious identity, where they can ask difficult questions, and where they can be allowed to be themselves and to be proud of their cultures. This is facilitated through small faith-sharing groups; however, the focus on diversity, dialogue, and cultural enrichment is one that is emphasized in the community as a whole. This has been done in numerous ways.

Outreach to Hispanic students has been carried out through tapping into practices of popular piety, namely, Dia de los Muertos (day of the dead) and the devotion to Our Lady of Guadalupe. As a student organization the Newman Catholic Club was invited to participate in the school's annual altar competition for Dia de los Muertos. Though Dia de los Muertos has increased in visibility in mainstream American culture, for many it had been reduced to sugar skull face painting and an association with Halloween, without any consideration of its religious significance as a celebration rooted in All Souls' Day. The center participated in the altar competition, creatively led by the Pastoral Universitaria faith-sharing group, with the intention of highlighting the religious roots and meaning of the festivity. The altar won first place in the competition, beating out all of the Greek organizations and other ethnic organizations that participated.

A bilingual mass is also held in the university union to celebrate the Feast of Our Lady of Guadalupe, and, despite falling in the middle of finals week, has been attended by over two hundred students each year. Masses that are held on campus or at the center for larger celebrations, such as Ash Wednesday, are celebrated bilingually as well.

Another form of outreach to Hispanic and other immigrant students has been through social-advocacy efforts. With immigration and racial tension currently at the forefront of American society, the center has been an outspoken supporter of comprehensive immigration reform as prescribed by the social teachings of the church. Recent changes to key immigration legislation, specifically Deferred Action for Childhood Arrivals (DACA), have affected many of our community members personally, either because they themselves are undocumented or because they have family members who are. The center has held press conferences and forums with Bishop Jaime Soto in support of all DACA recipients, collaborates with campus organizations with similar views, and also participates actively in community organizing and advocacy at the local and state levels.

Building a Dynamic Community of Students

The center's outspoken stance in support of immigrants was something that not all Newman students understood or agreed with. To address this, a night of dialogue was facilitated to discuss with the community the Catholic social teachings regarding immigration and to allow a space for sharing, questions, and discussion. The most powerful part of the evening was the testimony of a brave member of our student community who disclosed [his/her] immigration status for the first time and shared the difficulty and uncertainty that [he/she] faces every day. An issue that was once abstract was suddenly given a face—that of a charismatic, popular student leader who many considered a close friend. DACA recipients and undocumented immigrants were no longer just an anonymous group of people; they now included a member of the community with whom students shared life with on an almost daily basis.

The evening of dialogue had a huge impact on the community. Overall, the experience has enabled the students to identify the face of Christ in their neighbor—they are more sensitive to the plight of immigrant communities, and many have had their hearts moved into action. Many who previously remained silent on the issue now actively speak out on social media in support of immigration reform, and others are now involved with community organizing. Still others continue to struggle with it, yet they show up to advocacy events in support of their community members, putting politics and debates aside to focus on the people that they love.

In the Newman Catholic Center Sacramento's mere two years as a dedicated center for campus ministry, the leadership team has already doubled in size, showing that despite the many challenges the students face, they are willing to commit to service. The diversity of the community is also noteworthy, with participation of Hispanic and Asian students continuing to increase, making it more reflective of the diocesan and campus reality. Outreach to other cultural communities, such as Korean and Vietnamese students, is planned for upcoming years, and the student leadership envisions the center becoming a pioneer in intentionally diverse college campus ministry.

13

Building Solidarity through Love

Manhattan College

LOIS HARR AND JENNIFER ROBINSON

As a Lasallian Catholic institution, Manhattan College has a commitment to faith, service, and social justice. Research shows that an effective way to encourage people toward social justice and solidarity is to have them engage in significant experiences combined with reflections that move and change their hearts and their minds. "You can perform miracles by touching the hearts of those entrusted to your care."[1] These words of our founder, St. John Baptist de La Salle, are ultimately what every Lasallian educator strives to accomplish.

The Office of Campus Ministry and Social Action has provided such experiences through service trips for at least twenty years. As this program has grown and developed, we increasingly see the importance of small group experiences in touching the hearts of students.

For several years the mission trips or social-action trips were admittedly somewhat haphazard, few in number, and did not have consistent guiding principles. In January 2007 the stars aligned

---

[1] John Baptist de La Salle, *Meditations by John Baptist de La Salle*, ed. Augustine Loes and Francis Huether (Washington, DC: Lasallian Publications, 2007), 338–39.

and the college was able to organize a winter break trip to Ecuador with Rostro de Cristo. Coincidentally—or providentially—a new coordinator for social action, who had significant experience with immersion trips, began that same month. It quickly became apparent that creating a purposeful program with serious themes and substantial outcomes—and one that would spark genuine student interest—would also require an actual name, something well beyond "social-action trips."

Within the month and after several manipulations and acronyms involving the word *Lasallian,* the Lasallian Outreach Volunteer Experience (LOVE) was born. The newly hired coordinator expanded and developed the few existing service trips into a more structured and robust program. LOVE, as we know it today, offers students ten or more opportunities throughout the year to live and serve in marginalized communities domestically and abroad. LOVE is organized around four pillars: service and social justice, cultural immersion, community, and spirituality. LOVE seeks to transform students' hearts and minds by having them live in solidarity with the poor in an unfamiliar culture; learn about issues of social justice; engage in direct service; and reflect on the world in light of faith, spirituality, and their own experiences.

Growing in LOVE

When LOVE was first established, there were three to four trips offered annually, with minimal attention given to group dynamics. Over the years there has been a steady increase in both the number of trips and the number of students participating. By 2013, there were ten trips offered, with approximately one hundred students taking part each year.

In 2011, Manhattan College undertook a branding initiative coordinated by an outside consultant. The company's research with various campus constituents revealed that LOVE was one of the most familiar and highly regarded programs at the college. This outcome greatly encouraged the staff and students working on the project, and LOVE has since been highlighted in all admissions promotional materials as well as on the college website. Many students cite the LOVE program as a very significant factor in their decision to attend Manhattan College.

Another important development for LOVE was the expansion of the pool of advisers who help prepare and accompany students on the trips. In the beginning this pool was almost exclusively campus ministry and social action staff members and graduate assistants. By 2009 and 2010, colleagues from other administrative and academic areas began participating. At present, some trips require an application process and interviews for advisers. Like salt and leaven, this has helped LOVE permeate the campus culture.

Lessons for LOVE Groups before, during, and after Trips

The nonpartisan Christian citizens' movement to end hunger, Bread for the World, has published a resource entitled *Getting Ready to Come Back: Advocacy Guide for Mission Teams*. This one small booklet speaks to and clarifies significant lessons learned over the years: the need for preparation before a trip; regular timely reflection during a trip, and ongoing opportunity for reflection and action after a trip. If students return from a trip and the most significant things they share are, "They're poor, but they're happy," "We helped those people so much," "I helped make one person smile," or, "It makes me realize how grateful I should be," then the program has failed.

Preparation and critical reflection in teams and small groups is essential. Previously, student leaders had not been adequately equipped to prepare the students for their experience. This was a disservice to students and the partner organizations, and frankly, was irresponsible behavior. Students need to know some of the history of the location and the issues confronting the host communities, from the Lower Ninth Ward of New Orleans to Port-au-Prince,

Haiti, from the Blackfeet Reservation in Montana to slums in Nairobi, Kenya. They must not leave a site and return to campus feeling only pity or being self-congratulatory, never having learned about the underlying structural injustices that are closer to the real causes of the situations they encountered.

Regarding reflection, the program takes its cue from American philosopher and educator John Dewey: "We do not learn from experience. . . . We learn from reflecting on experience."[2] Dewey held that experience results in education, but that without careful, critical reflection, it may well actually be miseducation. It may result, for instance, in reinforcing negative stereotypes. Dewey teaches that reflection is the process of examining what has happened in order to extract meaning that can lead to intelligent dealing with further experiences. Critical reflection entails thoughtful consideration of assumptions or supposed knowledge and their underlying supports or proofs.

The Office of Campus Ministry and Social Action staff and those involved with LOVE have learned the importance of critical reflection in regard to various issues of justice and exploring each participant's own identity, experiences, faith, and beliefs. This is crucial before, during, and after a LOVE trip in order to learn and open one's mind to the experience, the people, and the injustices encountered. In this process we have discovered how important the small group dynamic is for fostering critical reflection and personal transformation.

Over the past several years we have also become aware of the links between the LOVE groups and the Lasallian tradition. The Institute of the Brothers of Christian Schools, founded as St. John Baptist de La Salle, saw the need to bring together teachers into communities to teach children on the margins of society. Brothers even take "vows of association" to recall the centrality of

---

[2] John Dewey, *How We Think: A Restatement of the Relation of Reflective Thinking to the Educative Process* (Lexington, MA: D.C. Heath, 1933), 78.

community to the Lasallian mission. In recent decades the documents of the institute have frequently encouraged lay partners and students to find ways of sharing in this spirit of association.

In light of this learning the staff addressed the need for tools and resources for pre-trip preparation and reflection. Within the last two years a LOVE syllabus has been developed for leaders to use to help facilitate students' growth and reflection. The syllabus outlines various social-justice topics deemed important for every student to learn regardless of trip destination. Topics include privilege and identity, charity and justice, poverty and inequality, and race and racism. The syllabus also includes selections on Lasallian heritage and Catholic social teaching as well as suggestions and examples of reflection tools such as activities and discussion prompts.

Once groups have returned from their experiences, they are required to attend a post-trip reflection. This event helps students process their experience and reflect on their transformation. Depending on what time of year the trips take place, some student groups will continue to meet. We have also organized a "How's your LOVE life?" gathering for students who have gone on trips. Some ways students have continued to keep their experience alive is through getting more involved with their church, volunteering in their local community, or engaging in organizing and advocacy work.

Do No Harm

A significant challenge every service immersion group must face is ensuring no harm is done to the people and communities visited, and that the experience is not wasting time or resources better spent elsewhere. Every effort is made to work with reputable organizations with longstanding commitments and relationships in the communities. We do not want to support or be perceived as endorsing any type of "service tourism." We therefore seek to work with organizations that employ local individuals and work on authentic, sustainable development and do not just provide charity.

This is especially true in the wake of a natural disaster, as students often want to pick up and go to help immediately. It is the responsibility of the staff, advisers, and experienced leaders to explain that LOVE must not be a burden to the organizations and people who have been devastated enough without the additional complication of well-meaning but unskilled visitors.

Program Structure

Each LOVE trip has its own team, usually no more than a dozen or so individuals. Each team has one or two student leaders and one or two professional colleagues who serve as advisers. At the beginning of each semester students are recruited through fliers, the college announcement portal, personal invitations, club fairs, and LOVE Night, which showcases upcoming trips. During LOVE Night students begin to discern which trip—and team—might be appropriate for them through posters, pictures, and personal stories from previous trip participants.

The number of students applying for each trip varies depending on the destination and time of year it is offered (winter, spring, or summer break). Typically, there are more applications than spots available for each trip. Staff and leaders strive to accommodate every applicant, but at times some students may be asked to defer and be considered for a future trip.

A LOVE student advisory board meets weekly. The function of the board is to discuss current and future trips, recruit and select student leaders, be a liaison to the student leaders, and work on fundraising events. Every effort is made to keep the costs of trips within reach for as many students as possible. Fortunately, and in a true Lasallian spirit, the college's Student Government provides approximately a 20 percent subsidy to the LOVE program from student activity fees.

An important organizational principle of LOVE is to make a Lasallian connection at home or abroad whenever possible. Additionally, since Manhattan College is a Catholic Relief Services Global Campus, for trips outside the United States an effort is made to connect with CRS as well. This principle helps determine which sites are picked as well as the structure and itinerary of trips on the ground.

For instance, LOVE Montana takes place at the DeLaSalle Blackfeet School in Browning, where Manhattan students live and work with the Lasallian community of brothers and volunteers. Similarly, since 2014, LOVE Haiti has partnered with the Lasallian school in Port-au-Prince and spends a day with CRS in the field.

The Power of the Small Group

Once teams are determined, they meet weekly for the semester prior to the trip. During these meetings leaders use the LOVE syllabus to prepare the group for the experience. Each week, participants engage in dialogue and reflection with their teammates.

A typical weekly meeting agenda might include an ice-breaker or warm-up activity, updates on trip details or fundraising progress, or an activity such as a short video or brief reading followed by reflection. Meetings end with a prayer, usually a CRS resource, and closing "I statements."

So, for instance, students may start with recalling a "rose, thorn, or bud" from the previous week: where there was beauty or joy, where there was pain or struggle, where there was hope. Students then may discuss trip finances, the schedule for a fundraising event later in the week, or plan a team-building dinner together.

The bulk of the meeting is reserved for the activity and reflection. The LOVE syllabus calls for every group to watch "The Danger of a Single Story," a TED Talk by Chimamanda Ngozi Adichie, as well as to read Ivan Illich's 1968 address "To Hell with Good Intentions."

These kinds of resources challenge students to examine their own assumptions, to recognize their own perspectives, and to begin to imagine from the perspective of another. Notions of charity and justice come into play, helping students uncover systemic injustice as they face the challenges of immediate charitable responses and the need for long-term, just solutions.

Meetings close with a prayer for understanding and solidarity followed by "I statements," which may be along the lines of "I feel . . . " (scared, uneasy, more informed, better prepared, worried about how I will handle things, unsure, glad I have my team, and so on).

The group dynamic continues during the trip itself. By then, students should have developed a sense of community that can better facilitate critical reflection of the experiences during nightly meetings. Following the trip, student groups will continue to meet, when possible.

What's Faith Got to Do with It?

Fostering an inclusive community is identified as a key value for Manhattan College. The LOVE program strives to be open, inclusive, and accessible to all members of the college community. Cost is an issue for some students. Not all students can afford the time and money needed to take part in the LOVE program.

Another significant philosophical challenge is ensuring that LOVE remains open to students and advisers regardless of their faith tradition (if they have one). This is made explicit throughout recruiting, as is the fact that one core pillar of LOVE is spirituality. All participants are invited to share in their own faith and life journeys and are required to be open to others' spiritual journeys as well. Typically, there is an exchange of prayers as well as a commissioning mass before the students attend the trips.

Most of LOVE's partner organizations are faith based, so prayers and religious services are almost always a part of every experience. Ironically, individuals have mixed reactions, with some declining to participate because LOVE is "too religious" and others observing that LOVE is not "Catholic enough." For most, however, it is an experience filled with meaning and purpose.

All the preparation outlined above is in service of the actual experience—the particular LOVE trip a student participates in and the impact it has on the parties involved. LOVE participants may do some physical work, such as helping to build a house, making repairs at an orphanage, or serving food in a soup kitchen. More often than not they listen, visit, laugh, interact, play, choke back tears, ask questions, and absorb. All of this becomes the focus of each evening's small group reflection.

The profound impact these experiences and communities have on our students can be seen in the ways in which students make significant changes to their lives. Some become vegetarians or start limiting their excessive water usage; some decide to volunteer in their local community; some decide to become Catholic or finish the sacraments of initiation through RCIA. Some students have even changed their career path. From being a finance major to studying economic development, or from a pre-law trajectory to working with college students in student engagement, or from a business marketing major to joining the Peace Corps, these transformative experiences have not only influenced them while on the trip, but also encouraged them to pursue their true vocation. One student in particular was studying chemistry and was set to pursue a career in the health field when she attended her first LOVE experience. As a participant in Ecuador and then as a student leader in Kenya her heart and mind were opened to the needs of the world and the realization that education was the key to overcoming poverty and oppression. She decided after graduating that she would, instead, become a long-term volunteer with the Lasallian Volunteers and teach chemistry in Racine, Wisconsin. She went on to pursue a master's degree in education and is currently teaching in a New York City public school.

In their small LOVE groups, using the methods and tools practiced throughout the course of their weekly meetings, the students and advisers share their reactions, their confusion, their questions, and their unfolding realizations about the day's events and encounters. While these gatherings are not technically or exclusively small Christian communities, they provide an opportunity to be vulnerable, to be honest, and to probe the human condition and find meaning. They provide an opportunity to come together, in a shared mission, and to connect faith to everyday life. For most, it is profoundly spiritual in nature.

The hope is that the experience of a LOVE trip for any participant will embody these words of the late Dean Brackley, SJ:

> If we listen attentively to their stories, we can begin to see our reflection in their eyes, hear our story in theirs, recognize our hidden struggle for life in their open struggle against death. In this way we let these strangers break our hearts. Solidarity is born.[3]

---

[3] Dean Brackley, SJ, *The Universtiy and Its Martyrs: Hope from Central America* (San Salvador: Universidad Centroamericana, 2005).

14

Ignite

Small Groups at Purdue University

ABIGAIL RUSKEY

In March 2013, I received all the sacraments of initiation through the St. Thomas Aquinas Catholic Center of Purdue University. I was only eighteen at the time and finishing up my first year as a college student in liberal arts. My conversion that year was a radical shift in my lifestyle; the only ministry I was involved with through St. Tom's, as we so affectionately call it, was its RCIA (Rite of Christian Initiation of Adults) program, where my entire world was rocked. I had been raised in a very anti-Catholic house-hold and grew up with friends who lead sinful lifestyles. My desire to convert happened when I was much younger, but my parents prohibited me from converting until I was out of the house and on my own. For me, this meant that my conversion at college would cause a rift in my family life and my personal life because I had to rid myself of toxic relationships and define my new self within my family. So in converting to Catholicism in March, I found that I was utterly alone. My RCIA instructor encouraged me to join one of the small groups from St. Tom's through its ministry, Ignite. These groups provided me with faithful, Catholic friends to encourage me in my journey, and they are still some of my great-est friends to this day. Without the Ignite small groups I would not have made it through my transition into the Catholic Church. Faith is not meant to be lived alone, and in my Ignite group, I discovered for the first time that I did not have to be alone.

Beginning my sophomore year at Purdue, I decided to lead my own small group through the Ignite ministry; it was here that our Lord called me into evangelization. As a group leader I noticed a common trend on the college campus. Catholic freshmen would step onto campus, away from their parents for the first time, and then be faced with a decision: Do I continue to live out this faith that I was raised in or do I drop it? Learning this, I invited anyone I could to my small group, recalling my own loneliness in the faith, hoping to give to others the community that would encourage them to say yes to the fullness of the Catholic faith, to the sacraments, and, above all, to Jesus Christ.

I believe that the Lord gave me the grace to create an atmosphere where students would encounter Jesus more profoundly, repent of their old lives, and believe in the gospel. Watching this process was a most intimate experience, like watching clay be formed into magnificent pottery before my eyes as I watched the Spirit breathe life again into decaying bones. I led Ignite groups until I graduated from Purdue. Through my leadership in Ignite, the Lord called me to give my entire self to small group evangelization in the ministry of FOCUS (Fellowship of Catholic University Students). I now implement this model of small Christian community life as a full-time apostolate. My whole week is dedicated to forming these communities on campus and letting the Spirit move within each of them. I cannot count the number of students that I have seen join small groups and have their lives utterly transformed in Ignite at Purdue and in FOCUS.

The Format of Ignite

Today, there are fourteen Ignite groups at Purdue. Most meet weekly in student dorms and draw students from those residence halls. In order to better respond to the needs of students, one group meets at a local bar; others meet at St. Tom's; one group is bilingual (English and Spanish); another is for those students involved in student fraternities and sororities.

Recruitment

The goal of Ignite is to give students an encounter with Jesus through the scriptures and offer them a community to help build up their lives upon Christ and his church. In order to accomplish this goal, students apply to be Ignite leaders and are selected based on their potential for leadership in the faith and their zeal for the scriptures and small group evangelization. These leaders receive training in small group leadership by The Evangelical Catholic, a nonprofit formation and training organization, over the summer at a training camp and then on a monthly basis throughout the year. Ignite groups are coed and take place in almost every dormitory on Purdue's campus. Two leaders are selected for each group, typically one male and one female, and the partners each select a day and time for their weekly meetings. During the St. Thomas Aquinas "Blockbuster Weekend," the primary fall outreach event at St. Tom's, the Ignite leaders collect names and numbers of interested students, and the leaders each contact the students living in a specific dorm and invite them into their small group. St. Tom's also does an excellent job of advertising the various Ignite times and locations for each small group so that throughout the year a student can find a specific group and join at any time.

Meeting Format

While each small group adds its own personality and specifications to a meeting, the typical Ignite meeting is a discussion of the gospel for the following Sunday. This way, students begin to center their lives upon the coming Sabbath, a symbol for the great Sabbath rest in eternity with our Lord. Small group leaders are trained in preparing solid questions, facilitating discussion, and fostering relationships during their time together as well as outside the weekly meetings. Each small group starts with a prayer followed by an opening question; many leaders use "God moments," where each member tells of a time he or she saw God during the week. I find God moments vital to the students' growth in faith, because the practice cultivates a longing in the heart to see Jesus, as Zacchaeus did (Luke 19:3).

The small group then reads aloud the gospel for that Sunday, and the leaders facilitate a group discussion based on the reading. At the end the leaders usually introduce a question or challenge designed to help students take their discussion of the gospel and infuse the ideas or discoveries into their daily life, lest they remain only ideas or new bits of information. By applying the insights from the discussion, the members of the small group align their lives to Christ's and leave transformed, pondering the gospel message throughout their week. Upon attending Sunday mass, the priest proclaims the very same gospel, solidifying the changes they have been ardently working on that week. The meetings end in a variety of forms of prayer; many leaders simply say a concluding prayer, thanking the Lord for graces received and petitioning for fortification throughout the week. I typically end small group discussions with a sort of intercessory prayer, offering every member the opportunity to speak his or her petitions aloud to the Lord. I have found that this format gives confidence to students who initially may be uncomfortable with praying aloud.

Leader Formation

The small group leaders receive their formation from The Evangelical Catholic. Throughout the year, however, each leader receives one-on-one mentorship from a more seasoned leader up the chain. A few students chosen as Ignite coordinators are formed directly by the campus minister; the coordinators oversee the structure and troubleshoot for leaders on the ground while also mentoring a handful of leaders. Other veteran leaders also take positions as small group mentors. Doing so ensures that everyone has the same vision and is being continually formed throughout the year in an intimate setting. This structure is still being worked out to find the best possible way to maintain time management as well as the consistency and quality of mentorship.

The Power of Small Groups

Through my experience with Ignite I have been transformed by the power of small groups. I am driven by the memory of my loneliness as a convert to the faith, rejected by my old community and uncertain if I would ever find another. I can say wholeheartedly that without Ignite through St. Tom's, I would not have the community that I do today and I certainly would not have been able to handle all that my conversion called me to forsake. I do not have a Catholic family by blood—but because of the friends I made in these small groups, I have an incredibly massive Catholic family in the body of Christ. It is an honor to call them my brothers and sisters.

15

From Small Church Communities to Vibrant Catholic Life at Yale University

ROBERT BELOIN

Campus ministry in service to the Catholic students and faculty of Yale University began in 1922 with the appointment of Fr. T. Lawrason Riggs as the first chaplain. Under the guidance of my six predecessors, there has been a concerted effort to respond to the various needs of both groups with creative and innovative initiatives.

When I was appointed chaplain in 1994, there were two Sunday masses, each half filled. If students wanted to pray in the chapel, they had to ring the doorbell during the day (9:00 a.m.–5:00 p.m.) to be let in by the secretary. There was no room for programs except in the chaplain's residence. The physical space limited what could be offered to students.

Through more than forty years in a priestly ministry, I approached a particular challenge by first asking the *what* question before I asked *how* to do it. If I don't have a comprehensive understanding of what I am trying to accomplish, all the activity would be "hit or miss," with no clear focus.

I found myself frequently asking what the Catholic center should look like in one of the great universities of the world. What I saw around me was not a very impressive answer to that question. The chapel and library, built in 1938, were only open during normal business hours, and were not available to students in the evening, when they would be most likely trying to use such spaces.

But more important than physical space, it was clear that we needed a new approach for helping students to gather in a meaningful way. In the course of many conversations I heard frequent themes: lack of vocabulary for talking about the Catholic faith; poor knowledge of scripture that became embarrassingly clear in conversations with evangelical Christians; and a frequent loneliness that surprised me, given the close proximity with others that students share on campus. These conversations brought home for me the need for a new approach to respond to their stated needs: knowledge of theology and scripture, and an experience of a supportive community.

In trying to meet these needs a basic decision had to be made: was the ministry to be structured along traditional lines where the needs of the community are met by the ordained, or was a different structure possible? The church of the twenty-first century is still hampered by a truncated approach to ministry that has been in our vocabulary for decades. Lay Catholic Action in the 1950s taught that the ordained were called to ministry and they "let" the laity participate in their ministry. The document on the laity in the Second Vatican Council corrected that teaching and declared that *all* the baptized are called to ministry (*Apostolicam Actuositatem*, no. 3). Thus, the foundation for ministry correctly shifted from ordination to baptism. The specific implication for pastoral ministry is for the ordained not to attempt to be the sole provider of ministry to a passive congregation but for the baptized to minister to one another with the support of the ordained. Therefore, I did not see myself as being the only one to minister to them; rather, my task was to form a community where they could actively minister to one another. One way of thinking about this structure is to encourage people not simply to *go to* church but to learn to *be* church for one another.

This insight came to life after about five years of promoting this initiative. An undergraduate who had joined a small church community (SCC) suffered the death of her father after a lengthy illness. My uncle happened to die at the same time. Since I had to attend my uncle's funeral, I was not able to go to her father's funeral in a neighboring state, as I ordinarily would have done. However, her entire SCC attended her father's funeral. When she returned to campus, she told me how supported she felt by the St. Thomas More community. I was delighted that she experienced such support even though I was not present. Her SCC was "church at the root" for her, and meaningful ministry was being done without my personal involvement. Her experience of church did not depend on me but was a gift given to her from those who ministered to her out of their baptismal calling. I saw my challenge as forming communities where people could minister to one another and not promote a structure where I was arrogantly the sole provider of ministry.

On our national scene, where there are fewer priests, it seems like a "no brainer" to approach ministry in such a way that the baptized laity are called forth to minister to one another with the help of the ordained, who have their own charism but need not see themselves as the sole providers of ministry. With a deeper appreciation for baptismal ministry, more people are involved and a deeper ministry is experienced.

When I came to campus, I had just completed three years as a member of the initial advisory board for the National Alliance of Parishes Restructuring into Communities, founded by Fr. Art Baranowski of Detroit. The core impetus was to help people connect life and faith on a regular basis and to build a more relational experience of church at the parish level—where church is not put on by a few for the many, but rather all are called to use their gifts and talents for the common good. Having been inspired by that vision of parish, my initial interest in campus ministry was to try to adapt the parish model to student life.

At the beginning of my third semester as chaplain, in January 1996, I presented the community not with a program but rather a way of restructuring the community. I invited students and faculty to join an SCC once the academic schedule was finalized for the semester. At that point they would know if they were free on a Wednesday or Thursday evening to be able to take part. On "Sign Up Sunday" everyone was invited to join a group of eight to twelve members. The groups would use a journal that the leadership team had prepared. The journal included the first reading and the gospel for the coming Sunday, a commentary on both texts, and reflection questions to begin a conversation. The journal also included suggestions for how to carry any insights from this discussion into their daily lives in the coming week. This section, "Response in Action," then became the first thing that was discussed at the beginning of the next meeting. Having had this discussion, the question needs to be asked: "So what? Having shared these ideas, what impact will it have on the way I live when I leave here?"

Our approach here emphasizes lectionary-based faith sharing rather than a Bible study program. Some campuses might offer "bible study" where students meet to discuss a particular book of the Bible, but their worship experience is not connected to it. Others study the Gospel according to Mark, for example, and then come to mass on Sunday and have a reading from the Gospel according to Luke. Our journal includes readings for the coming Sunday so that what happens in the SCC prepares for and enhances the experience of the large church community that meets at Sunday mass. The Sunday liturgy means more to students when they have read and studied the readings before they come to mass.

After every meeting a member of each community is asked to write a summary of the discussion and any unresolved issues on the back of the attendance sheet and leave it in a designated box at the front desk. I read these summaries as part of my homily preparation, and it is amazing how many times I've changed my homily to respond to the questions that surfaced in a particular

SCC. I sometimes refer to a point made in an SCC as part of my homily, and in that way the discussion from an SCC becomes connected to the large church community at worship.

The greatest challenge in promoting a vision of SCC is the complex schedules of students and faculty. In addition to a very demanding academic schedule, students are involved in a variety of extracurricular activities. At the beginning of the academic year an Activities Fair offers students a chance to sign up for a wide variety of activities. There are over four hundred options, and so making time for an SCC along with all the demands of the academic schedule and extracurricular activities is a daunting challenge. We frequently remind students that an SCC is not just another extracurricular activity or another program to join; rather, it is how we structure ourselves as a community to make growing in faith a priority.

It is very inspiring to see students mature in their faith through involvement in an SCC. Members of the group take turns leading the discussion for the evening as a way for each member to take ownership for the vitality of the group. Part of the genius of Catholicism is its appreciation for pastoral connections. As the pastor connects the parish to the diocesan church, and the bishop connects the diocesan church to the universal church, so a pastoral facilitator connects an SCC to the pastor and the mission of the larger parish. In a parish those individuals would be called pastoral facilitators, acknowledging that they share the task of pastoring the parish. It was interesting to see a pastor's attempt to implement this vision of parish but hesitate to call the people pastoral facilitators; he called them only facilitators. It was a clue that he did not really see them as helping him pastor the parish. They were only facilitators of groups. Since St. Thomas More is not a canonical parish but a chapel—I am not a pastor; I am a chaplain—the standard vocabulary does not fit. Therefore, each group identifies a pastoral liaison to serve as a connection between the individual SCC and the larger community in order to include that aspect in the structure of this initiative. I meet with this group twice a semester, over dinner, to discuss confidentially what is happening in the groups. At one meeting a pastoral liaison reported that the material we had provided on centering prayer seemed like New Age material to one member. I was able to provide background material on centering prayer that could be brought back to the group for clarification. At this meeting we also receive helpful feedback on what improvements they would like to see in the journal for the following semester.

In 1997, I invited Kerry Robinson to join the pastoral team as the chapel's director of development. Together, we expanded the program offering for students and raised the funds to build a center that would house our expanding program. To help students appreciate their Catholic faith more deeply, we began to offer a robust schedule of speakers throughout the academic year. There are three endowed fellowships, four endowed lectureships, and a guest speaker at every Sunday dinner. I especially appreciate one particular initiative—Life as a Scholar and a Believer—in which we invite the Catholic faculty to speak about their faith and how their faith affects their work. On many occasions it is the only time an undergraduate is able to hear from a particular professor, and it is always inspiring for undergraduates to hear faculty say how important their faith is to their life. With their inspiring witness, students experience that it's OK to be Catholic on Yale's campus.

In 2006, the 30,000-square-foot Thomas E. Golden Jr. Center was dedicated. This student center was intended as an expansion of the old Catholic chapel. The center was designed by Cesar Pelli. Tom was an important collaborator with us as we articulated what we hoped to accomplish by expanding the Catholic chapel on the campus of Yale University. As a successful Connecticut businessman, he helped us to refine our goals and to be clear in what we were trying to accomplish with this stunning new center. Today, most of the SCC meetings are held in the center on virtually every night of the week. With its large public spaces and smaller, more intimate spaces it has become the focal point of Catholic life on campus. On most evenings the building is open until midnight, and students meet for their SCC, study in the library, relax in the rec room, and enjoy the company of their friends in various other rooms. The center, and the activities of so many students within it, is a powerful witness to the fact that Catholic life has come of age on campus as students learn to connect life and faith on a regular basis.

One of the challenges of having provided this experience to students during their bright college years, however, is to help them transition to parish life after graduation. In collaboration with the Leadership Roundtable, St. Thomas More initiated the ESTEEM (Engaging Students to Enliven the Ecclesial Mission) program. ESTEEM offers students an opportunity to meet during the academic year and discuss ideas about ecclesiology, canon law, social justice, and spirituality. By 2016, this initiative was on twelve college campuses across the country. One graduate sent me an email that summarized the challenges that he faced after graduation: "Father, I keep looking for a parish where I can become involved. The parishes I have visited are geared to parents with small children and senior citizens. I sorely miss my SCC." If he saw "sign up for a young adult SCC" in the parish bulletin, he would be there in a heartbeat. Unfortunately, many parishes have not embraced this structure for parish life.

It is my hope that more and more Catholic parishes and campus ministry communities will make the decision that reflects these basic core principles:

1. Within the large community, form small communities where everyone is invited to minister to others because they are baptized;
2. Prepare for the Sunday assembly by studying the readings beforehand;
3. Build a more relational church;
4. Help one another learn to see the connections between life and faith on a regular basis and thus recognize God's presence in our lives;

5. Structure ourselves so that we learn not just to *go to* church but to *be* church for one another.

Such is the challenge before us. If this is the *what* we are doing, we will continue to discover ever more creative and effective ways in *how* to do it.

Epilogue

Discovering Christ
in Our Small Communities

EDOUARD KAROUE AND EVELINA MANOLA

Breaking open the Word of God in Scripture, we discover the centrality of love in the teachings of Jesus Christ: "I give you a new commandment, that you love one another. Just as I have loved you, you also should love one another. By this everyone will know that you are my disciples, if you have love for one another" (John 13:34–35). Followers of Christ, no matter what the age, are meant to witness to Christ through love; Christians are called to be Christ in the world. In the history of the Catholic Church an important way that Christians have done this is through the creation and participation in communities and movements, from the house churches and Benedictine monasteries of early Christianity to the small Christian communities that are featured in this book.

At the end of the nineteenth century, as a greater number of students gained access to higher education, Catholic college students began to create small communities to better enable them to witness to Christ's love in the university world. For many students, the drive to a community experience led them to create national and international networks of small communities. One of the earliest of these initiatives, of course, is FUCI, described in Chapter 2.

165

Inspired by Pope Leo XIII's *Rerum Novarum* and other texts of Catholic social teaching, Catholic students have also sought to witness to God's love and make a difference in the world on campus and beyond. After the First World War, FUCI and other movements of Catholic students sought to build a student movement for peace and created what would later be known as the International Movement of Catholic Students—Pax Romana (IMCS). For nearly a century this movement of, for, and by students has sought to evangelize the student milieu through the formation of small student communities.

Today, as we see in this book, Catholic students around the world are organizing themselves into communities of love that seek to bridge, in various ways, reflection, prayer, social action, and spirituality. Some of these are connected to larger communities, including IMCS, the Christian Life Community, and Evangelical Catholic. Others are standalone. Some are connected to a local parish or a religious congregation. Others are centered on lectionary readings or the Review of Life method. Still others have developed their own way of operating. Some are supported by large budgets with full-time staff members; others are almost entirely student run with limited funds. Some are exclusively Catholic; others are open to all students.

Despite these differences, it is in and through these communities that many students discover Christ and the transformative power of God's love. Often, this experience can be more profound than large experiences of church. Reading the accounts presented in this volume, we can appreciate how Christ is present in small faith groups of students in different ways: as a teacher, thinker, leader, and change maker.

Communities of Teachers

We can see Jesus, during his evangelical life, listening, praying, and teaching. Small campus faith communities often become communities of learning and teaching as students gather to deepen their understanding of their faith and of the world around them. A small faith group of students should be a space where students can learn from one another, from the gospel, and from the Catholic social tradition about what it means to be a Christian in the world today. Reading the weekly gospel and other texts from the Bible provide one space for us to learn and teach one another. Occasionally, this will also mean workshops, trainings, outside speakers, and retreats. The exposure programs used by AICUF or the service trips by Manhattan College's LOVE program are good examples of experiential learning that can take place with small student groups.

Students in small communities do more than just learn, however; they serve as teachers to one another. They witness to the gospel by serving as good examples to other students, taking care of their social and political environment. Being a teacher in a community, of course, demands, as Fr. Healey emphasizes in Chapter 2, that we listen to one another. Critical knowledge, as we know, comes from a mutual dialogue between teachers and learners. Small faith communities are doing just that.

Communities of Thinkers

Reading the life and teachings of Jesus, we see a man who engaged the intellectual debates of his time and who invited those around him, including the doctors of law, to think. Despite his youth, he showed greater wisdom than the elders of his community. This experience should challenge students today to connect the truth of God's love in the gospel to their intellect and to the reality of their world. For college and university students the call of the gospel has a specific sound. It must call us to think critically in the face of the ideologies that threaten social cohesion and human dignity. It calls us to think beyond ourselves.

In the face of a globalized society where many forces push for a culture of consumption and individualism, small student groups must encourage students to think critically and reevaluate contemporary values in the light of faith. Catholic student communities show the potential to create open minded and critical thinkers. Groups like the CRS Campus Ambassadors program, discussed in Chapter 9, are helping students to reconsider the dominant narratives of a consumer culture. They are building and empowering critical and open-minded leaders through transdisciplinary discussions centered on values.

Forming diverse multicultural communities creates valuable spaces for students to think more critically. As several authors (including Ahern, Flores, and Cichello) mention in this volume, our work with small student communities needs to attend to issues of cultural diversity. Larger church structures can help in this regard as they offer student communities what Fr. Beloin describes in Chapter 15 as "pastoral connections." Global networks like IMCS can connect students, like those in Mali or India, with their peers in different parts of the world. Critical thinking can also come as we tap into the diversity of different fields of study. An engineering student, for instance, may have a very different view of an issue from a sociology student. Putting them together in the same small group can be a learning experience, especially when centered on the gospel as a common basis.

Communities of Leaders

The concept of leadership, from what Jesus demonstrates, involves gratuity, service, community, and humility. He was concerned with the marginalized and witnessed to a greatness found in humble service. In many ways the crucifixion shows how threatened those in power were by his leadership.

Small Catholic student communities are important spaces to nurture leadership, as many of the chapters in this book show. But this is not just any kind of leadership; it is an ethical and empowered leadership. The way Catholic students organize themselves enables the establishment of good practices in leadership starting from empowerment, service, and a democratic way of governing. Student-led groups, as envisioned by the Second Vatican Council, may make mistakes, but these can be lessons in leadership (*Apostolicam Actuositatem*, no. 12).

If one the biggest problems, as Pope Francis writes in *Laudato Si'*, is that people today have "not been trained to use power well," then the university, as the great step in the preparation for professional life, becomes a crucial space for leadership formation (no. 105). Small groups become important places to help students realize their mission in society and to discover the real purpose of the studies. As Pope Francis stated in his visit to the Pontifical Catholic University of Ecuador, it is important "not to see a university degree as synonymous with higher status, money and social prestige." Rather, higher education must be seen as "a mark of greater responsibility in the face of today's problems, the needs of the poor, concern for the environment."[1] Small groups are important ways to help students make those connections.

Communities of Change Makers

The life and teaching of Christ shows the importance of love bearing fruit in action (Matt 7:24; James 2:26). Jesus was far from passive or indifferent to the realities of the world. He was a change maker. As Pope Francis points out, "Jesus does not hold back; instead, he gets involved in people's pain and their need. . . . *Compassion* leads Jesus to concrete action: *he reinstates the marginalized!*"[2] As several of the chapters here show, student

---

[1] "Pope Francis Address to the Pontifical Catholic University of Ecuador," Quito (July 7, 2015).

[2] Pope Francis, "Homily of His Holiness Pope Francis" (February 15, 2015).

communities, especially those grounded in the spirituality of action, are ways for students to get involved with others and make changes for the common good.

Among other things, this book highlights the capability of student communities to form leaders and change makers. Consider the very different ways that Marina D'Costa (India), Afou Chantal Bengaly (Mali), and Abigail Ruskey (United States) describe their experiences (Chapters 5, 6, and 14). These three young women have been empowered by their small community experiences to become leaders. For Bengaly and D'Costa, who come from contexts where Christians are a minority, this is a powerful sign of the potential of student movements.

As communities of teachers, thinkers, leaders, and change makers, small faith communities help students to discover Christ more fully. We know that when we gather in his name, Christ is present in our midst (Matt 18:20). It is in these spaces that students can learn about love, authentic relationships, justice, peace, and equity. It is the way many of us discover our vocations and what we can offer, even in small ways, to both the church and to humanity as a whole.

Today's world, as we know, is full of paradoxes. We are increasingly connected, but we communicate less. We have more goods, but we demand more from our limited planet. We can see the suffering of others on social media, but we remain indifferent to their plight. Students are thirsty for community and solidarity, but engendering commitment becomes difficult in the face of individualism and consumerism. In the face of these paradoxes and the many "structures of sin" that wound our planet today, we need more communities of all sizes and at all levels (local, national, global) to better witness to the love of Christ. These communities, when animated by the gospel and the Holy Spirit, can become "structures of grace" in a world marked by division and sin.[3] As

---

[3] See Kevin Ahern, *Structures of Grace: Catholic Organizations Serving the Global Common Good* (Maryknoll, NY: Orbis Books, 2015).

all university students know, there is a lot of noise in the world and there are many distractions that take us away from God's love. Alone, we have no chance to be heard, and it will be difficult to discover our true vocation. We need community—Love demands it. Christ demands it.

Appendixes

RESOURCES FOR SMALL STUDENT GROUPS

Appendix 1

Small Groups Field Guide

Catholic Campus Ministry Association

Small student faith-sharing groups are increasingly common on college campuses and many campus ministries place them in the center of all that they do. Some campuses call them Christian Life Communities while others refer to them simply as small groups. Whatever the name, this field guide will explain why so many Catholic campus ministry programs are using small groups and seeing great results.

Overview

This field guide is designed for campus ministry programs that want to begin using small groups. It may also be helpful for campuses that already offer small groups but can benefit from a refresher.

First, in Chapter 1, we'll define terms like "small groups" and distinguish between a small group and a Bible study. From there, in Chapter 2 we ask, "what's the point?" In other words, if small groups are simply opportunities for young people to gather and hang out, couldn't they do that in another setting? Small groups, especially in a Catholic campus ministry setting, are much more than just opportunities to socialize.

What do small groups look like on different campuses? How small is too small? How often should they meet? These questions and more are explored in Chapter 3. Chapter 4 examines the places that small groups can lead such as a greater expression of prayer and service.

Finally in Chapter 5, we look at the resources and next steps available to you related to small groups.

We hope that you find this field guide helpful as you continue to reach students for Christ and the Church.

Michael St. Pierre, Ed.D.
Executive Director, CCMA

1. Introduction: All in a Name

Small groups are known by many terms within the context of Catholic campus ministry. They are known around the country as:

- *Small Groups*
- *Christian Life Groups*
- *Christian Life Communities*
- *Cell Groups*
- *Small Christian Communities*
- *Campus Small Groups*
- *Student Groups*

One university describes their approach to small groups as a point of connection, enabling students to "bond, pray, and explore our faith and vocations." Another university describes small groups as a "great way to grow deeper in your relationship with God and others who share your Catholic faith." Often utilized as a way to make college "feel smaller," student groups forge deep bonds for students who can otherwise become anonymous.

One mid-west university describes their approach to small groups as having three pillars: spirituality, community and mission. Through weekly meetings, students gather to pray, talk and explore "where they have found God in their lives." Often, in Jesuit institutions, the concept of finding God "in all things" takes expression through small groups. By inviting students to reflect on God's presence in everyday life, their busy schedules find spiritual grounding.

Another university makes a direct link between personal discipleship with Christ and the small group: "Small groups are a great way to get to know Jesus while gaining relationships with other students." The focus on encountering Christ via small groups is essential and avoids what some call "bellybutton-gazing."

Some campus ministries place particular focus on discernment within small groups. This serves two purposes. First, it reminds students of their higher call as disciples of Christ. Second, it eases the transition to life after college. One university uses small groups to "help young adults learn how to make decisions according to God's will."

2. What's the Point of Small Groups?

Are small groups meant for studying the Bible? Do they facilitate discussions of faith? Can they prepare students for the upcoming Sunday Mass? Or, are they similar to support groups? One's perspective on the purpose of small groups will shape the answers to these questions. This chapter will bring clarity to the simple question that begins our journey—what's the point?

Small groups often serve two vital purposes within campus ministry:

1. Small groups act as an entry point to the campus ministry program.
2. Small groups provide a "discipleship path" for students that enables them to grow and deepen their relationship with Christ.

Small groups, when understood this way, are much more than just another program to offer. Rather, they have the potential to supercharge campus ministry such that students are continually "entering" campus ministry and maturing in their relationship with Christ.

It can be tempting, through no fault of any one person, for a campus ministry program to become insular. One campus minister put it this way, "I'm just happy if students show up for events." As students participate in events, we gain a certain satisfaction and a sense that our work is paying off. Students "showing up" can become the only measure of success.

This is a natural posture. Those serving in parishes can relate to this as well. If people show up on Sundays for Mass, that's certainly a good thing. *The catch is that it's not the only thing.*

For campus ministry programs to excel, it is imperative to "onboard" students regularly. This can take the form of a start-of-the-year cookout or a free concert. Small groups can also serve this purpose. Through regular invitations to join small groups, campus ministers keep the doors open for new students to take another step in their discipleship and faith.

Small groups also provide a practical way to help students mature in their faith. The weekly Mass experience can accomplish this but the environment is much larger and depends heavily on the quality of the preaching. Small groups are more manageable and get students talking. They provide accountability and tap into how young adults learn.

Three Tiers of Small Groups

Whether your campus ministry is promoting small groups or barely getting traction with them, there are three common stages of growth. These stages can be temporary or persist for several years:

Tier One: Small groups are not yet meeting but the campus ministry program has a desire to offer these in the future. A campus ministry may be in Tier One because of:

- Too many other programs in place.
- Not enough training on how to run small groups.
- A feeling that the staff is already stretched too thin.

Many times, campus ministry programs in Tier One feel as if small groups are just "one more thing" to coordinate. Even still, they know that small groups work but just can't seem to fit them into everything else that they currently offer. This can be due to an incomplete understanding of the value of small groups or due to a lack of planning.

Tier Two: Small groups are currently meeting but there isn't a plan for what comes next. Campus ministry programs in this tier have made some commitment to small groups but aren't totally sure what level of prominence small groups should play in the life of the ministry. Should every student be in a small group? *Should we "push" small groups? What if I don't have enough strong leaders to facilitate small groups? These questions and more are very common.*

Tier Three: Small groups are meeting and going according to plan. Students are moving along a discipleship path and inviting new students into groups. Evangelization and conversion are taking place. Campus ministries may be here for any number of reasons, such as:

- Dynamic leadership.
- Ample staffing to help student leaders.

Wherever you are on this scale, the key is to move your ministry a bit further. We are looking for progress, not perfection. Even for a Tier Three program, there is plenty of room for growth.

3. What Do They Look Like?

At Drew University in New Jersey, small groups look different from those at the University of Notre Dame in Indiana. Whether you look at Catholic institutions, public universities or commuter colleges, no two small groups are alike. By their nature, they aspire to be intimate, giving a campus ministry program a vehicle to make the Church feel small. What follow are some common elements of small group initiatives around the country.

Size

Small groups typically do not grow larger than 7–9 participants. The thinking is that bigger than nine becomes hard to manage. If one person cannot make the meeting time, you still have six to seven participants which can make for a dynamic and fruitful conversation. If a group is growing, it may be time to split it into two separate groups. This would then require a second facilitator. While the exact size of a group isn't etched in stone, a general rule is this: If it feels too big, it probably is.

Frequency

Most ministry programs suggest that groups meet once per week. Less frequently than once a week can leave students feeling disconnected. The value of a weekly gathering is that of training the muscle of small group accountability. By offering small groups weekly, students begin to crave the community they enjoy through a small group. The frequency makes it easy to remember and more effective in terms of building community.

Gender

Once again, campus programs differ in terms of their philosophy towards male-female small groups. The argument for single-gender groups is that they encourage more discussion on a very frank level. Along those lines, some campuses feel that men and women open up more often to those of the same gender, relating to one another on a deeper level than in a coeducational setting. On the other hand, some campuses find value in mixed-gender small groups. The argument in favor of coeducational groups is found in an appreciation for the faith perspective of someone from another gender. Whichever approach you choose, you'll want to think this through before launching small groups. What works on one campus might be different from the next.

Undergraduate or Graduate?

There appears to be less diversity in this regard. Most campuses encourage small groups for their undergrads and separate groups for their graduate students. At least one campus with an extensive small group program offers freshmen-only groups followed by sophomore-senior groups. The thought is that freshmen have unique issues and challenges that other students do not have.

Location

The location of a small group is quite important. Sometimes the easiest place for a small group to meet is the Catholic Center, the Newman Center or the campus ministry office. Typically, these locations have comfortable seating and small settings for quiet conversations.

Small groups do not have to be limited to "churchy" locations. They can take place in dorms, outdoors or even in the student center. Some campuses deliberately train their small group leaders to meet in locations that might be seen as "ordinary" such as a dorm or in a dining hall. This demonstrates a belief that Christians are the church and apply the words of Christ to their entire campus, "Wherever two or more are gathered, there I am in their midst" (Matthew 18:20).

Lectionary-based

As Catholics are familiar with the weekly rhythm of the Lectionary via Sunday Mass readings, many campuses utilize the Lectionary for small groups. This provides a "ready-made" curriculum to draw from as the Gospel reading in particular is a perfectly sized snippet of text on which students can reflect. The upside of a Lectionary-based approach to small groups is that Catholics are already familiar with it and the Lectionary provides more than enough material with which to work.

Another advantage of a Lectionary-based approach is the low barrier of entry. Catholics are familiar with how the readings are integrated into worship so talking about the readings prior to a Sunday Mass is an effective way to connect "Sunday with Monday."

A Lectionary-based approach is also quite affordable. No special books or materials are needed, just the Sunday Gospel reading. Our list of resources at the end of this Field Guide provide a number of user-friendly tools for a Lectionary-based approach to small groups.

Curriculum-based

Instead of a Lectionary-based approach to small group discussion content, some campuses prefer to use a set curriculum. This may come in the form of a booklet or even through video. The advantage of a curriculum-based model is that it can be topical, allowing groups to delve deep into one particular issue. A disadvantage is that the group can feel reliant on the "book," detracting from the organic vibe of a small group's maturation and spiritual development.

Are Small Groups the Same as a Bible Study?

Some people equate small groups with Bible studies. A Bible study can occur within a small group (and often does) but small groups, by our definition, are more than Bible studies. While a Bible study is often focused on "covering material," small groups are about making disciples in the context of a small community.

Format

Small groups run from 1–1.5 hours each week. A typical format often includes:

- Opening prayer: student facilitator
- Recap of the week: group ·
- Short reading: student (Bible)
- Discussion: group, led by the student facilitator
- Prayer intentions and pastoral needs: group.

Food is a "secret weapon" of any successful small group. Having snacks to offer at the beginning of small groups (or at the conclusion) helps to break the ice and make everyone feel welcome.

4. Where Can Small Groups Lead?

Small groups lead students to deeper friendship with Christ, to collegiality among its members and to a love of serving the poor. With the Holy Spirit as one's guide, small groups can be a powerful launching point for greater missionary discipleship.

A Means to an End

Small groups are a means to an end. While this may be obvious, there is a temptation for campuses to see certain aspects of ministry as an end in and of itself. Often, you'll see this with retreats. You can spot this mindset when someone says, "We can't change the retreat talk outline. We've used that one for over a decade!" *Really?*

Small groups can fall into this trap too. We can be so consumed with the format and models that we use that we forget that they are always a means to an end. When they become insular and self-focused, they lose their impact. On the other hand, when small groups are running effectively, they can be a powerful vehicle for the Holy Spirit to impact lives and for campus ministry to flourish. With that said, how far can small groups go? To which ends can they lead? What follow are some of the dramatic effects of small groups.

Missionary Discipleship

Small groups encourage students to grow in their personal relationship with Christ. When one is actively growing in his relationship with Jesus, he is naturally drawn to share his faith with others and serve those in need. Students find themselves reading the Bible more often in between group meetings and praying on their own more consistently.

Authentic Friendship

Deep friendships can form as a result of small groups. Students begin to count on one another for encouragement and support. They "nudge" one another forward in faith, offering prayer support and personal example. Authentic friendship stands in stark contrast to the faux-friendship often promoted via social media. Instead of having 500 "Facebook friends," small groups provide members with four, five, or even six truly authentic friends that they can count on.

Pastoral Care

No campus ministry staff can minister effectively to the hundreds or thousands of students on a college campus. Through small groups, students learn to minister to one another, thus extending the "reach" of the campus ministry staff. When a student needs help or is going through a difficult time, it's often the members of the small group that minister most effectively to their peers.

Service

Small groups can lead to greater expressions of service. A group may decide to participate together in a corporal act of mercy on a regular basis or spontaneously. Members of small groups encourage one another and share their stories of how the Lord is expanding their vision to include those most vulnerable and in the margins of society.

Retreats

Small groups are also a great way to promote upcoming events and invite other students to participate in retreats. Campus ministry programs find no lack of interest for retreats when a small group initiative is in place—a committed audience is always available. When a campus ministry program has small groups in place, their retreat program often has no trouble filling up.

Greater Connection to the Rest of Campus Ministry

Small groups can often form the glue of a campus ministry program. Communication can flow from the campus ministry program to small groups. Then, small group facilitators can "relay" back to campus ministry issues or needs that students have. Instead of relying on an email or a series of texts to communicate to students on campus, the campus ministry program can use its small group facilitators to share news of an upcoming event or ministry opportunity. A small group can also give the campus ministry program a vehicle for addressing difficult issues or campus scenarios that require more discussion than what a Sunday Mass homily can afford.

Social Events

Small groups also enable students to get together outside of the scheduled weekly meeting. This gives participants opportunities for fun and also moments to be with students who aren't (yet) plugged into campus ministry.

Reflection on Church Teaching

Finally, small groups can equip students to have deeper reflection on Church teaching. When a group is discussing a tough issue, there's no better reference than Church teaching. A skilled student facilitator can help a group connect daily life with the teachings of the Church.

5. Resources

Chapter 5 provides resources for getting going with small groups. Whether your campus already uses small groups or needs a jumpstart to take them to the next level, this provides you with a toolbox that you can take with you after you've finished studying the Field Guide. [Simply search in your web browser for the items listed below:]

- USCCB Daily Mass Readings & Reflections
- USCCB Campus Small Groups Resources
- USCCB App
- CCMA App
- Ascension Press
- 3 Quick Tips to Improve Your Small Groups
- Ascension Presents Video Series with Fr. Mike Schmitz
- Renew International: CampusRenew
- Fruitful Discipleship: Living the Mission of Jesus in the Church and the World (by Sherry Weddell)
- St. Paul's Outreach
- Small Christian Communities International Website
- America Magazine
- "When it Comes to Nurturing Faith, Smaller is Often Better"
- Evangelical Catholic
- Why Small Groups video
- Group Discussion Guides
- FOCUS Small Group Resources
- Steubenville Fuel Small Group Resources

Conclusion

This field guide would not be possible without the generous support of our benefactors. For more Catholic campus ministry resources, visit www.ccmanet.org.

Appendix 2

The Sunday Gospel

*Center Point for the
Campus Small Christian Community*

ROBERT MORIARTY, SM

So, what is the campus Small Christian Community (SCC) all about?

Is it a break from studies, a happy gathering with a small group of friends, a religious support group, a chance to connect more richly to Catholic stuff?

The SCC certainly provides these things and, if truth be told, there are real values at stake in each of these things.

But the SCC is about something essentially more.

For many, the SCC begins as a chance to slow down, a chance to notice one's life more closely, an opportunity to check priorities, a time to sift and sort the things that count, and yes, a chance to become more in touch with the presence and action of God in one's life, even if that is something one is not that aware of day by day, much less hour to hour.

But there is still something essentially more.

At its core, the full-fledged SCC comes together centered on the word of God, the scriptures of the upcoming Sunday, especially the gospel of the week. The SCC gathers to *hear the Lord's gospel* and to *hear the gospel's Lord—together*. And so, having spent time in reflection, conversation, and prayer, members prepare themselves to enter more fully into the weekly celebration of Eucharist, that place where we are above all formed by word and sacrament.

If the SCC orients us to more fully participate in the Eucharist, the Eucharist orients us to mission. Looking at our lives and the world through the lens of the gospel, we discover resonances that invite us to active response.

The gospel account of the flight of Joseph, Mary, and Jesus into Egypt, for instance, can attune us more keenly to the plight of immigrants in today's world and summon us to their support. The story of the rich young man might be allowed to challenge the possessiveness with which we hang on to things and move us to share our goods more generously with those in need. Jesus's injunction to his disciples to forgive "seventy-times-seven" might move us to engage more actively with peacemaking initiatives.

Orienting Ourselves to the Small Christian Community Gathering

One campus ministry is specific about encouraging its SCC members to deliberately take some minutes to recollect themselves, even to read over the gospel for the upcoming Sunday, before rushing off to their SCC gathering as if it is just another program, the next thing on an otherwise busy schedule.

This is an important piece of guidance, a valuable habit to get oneself into.

As already hinted, a twofold dynamic may be seen to be at work in the SCC gathering: (1) hearing the Lord's gospel; and (2) hearing the gospel's Lord. The first calls for us to attend to the gospel text itself. It involves reflection and conversation. The second calls for individual and communal prayer. It involves substantial silence.

There is a special disposition called for in order to enter genuinely into this dynamic, one which is a real challenge for many in the SCC. There is something of a spontaneous inclination among many of us to think that we come together in an SCC primarily to talk, to speak about our lives, about our faith, about God.

In *Sharing the Journey*, his otherwise appreciative study of the small group movement (mostly church-based groups) in the United States, Robert Wuthnow suggests that the occupational hazard of people in small groups in an individualistic culture is that many people come together, in effect, simply "to talk about themselves in the presence of others."[1]

Speaking—about our lives, about our faith, about God—is indeed a characteristic of the SCC experience. But a focus on the SCC dynamic as *hearing the Lord's gospel* and *hearing the gospel's Lord*, suggests that there needs to be a priority emphasis on *listening*—listening not only to our lives and one another's lives, but listening above all to God's word, by attending to the gospel and to God's Spirit stirring, even groaning, in our hearts and in our midst. In SCC, we do this listening personally and together.

Listening, genuinely hearing, calls for us to be capable of *silence*, personal silence and communal silence. Being able to be together in silence is a great gift that SCC members can give to one another. Along with cultivating rich conversation, SCCs serve the experience well by integrating generous opportunities for silence into the time of the small community's gathering.

To be formed by God's word we need first to be able to hear God's word. Listening in the quiet, listening together, is a real challenge in this busy, noisy world of ours.

There are many other important things that can be said about the SCC experience, but we concentrate here on the grounding point. We gather in SCC to center ourselves on the gospel, to allow ourselves to be formed by God's word, to animate us to work for God's reign, and to support one another in doing so.

---

[1] Robert Wuthnow, *Sharing the Journey: Support Groups and the Quest for a New Community* (New York: Free Press, 1994), 3.

Making Things More Concrete

What follows here is an adapted presentation of a suggested format for the weekly SCC. It was prepared originally for *Quest*, the Sunday-scripture resource for SCCs published by the Pastoral Department for Small Christian Communities (Archdiocese of Hartford).

At one level, the session format models an exercise of practical theological reflection. At another, and more grounding level, this format offers what might be called an encounter model for the small community centered on the twofold movement: hearing the Lord's gospel and hearing the gospel's Lord. For those familiar with lectio, this format might also be considered to be communal Lectio Divina.

To hear the Lord's gospel, one needs to hear the Lord, of course. And to hear the gospel's Lord means hearing the gospel. While those two dynamics are surely both at play at one and the same time, the actual experience of the small community session unfolds in two movements. The first part of the session focuses on hearing the Lord's gospel, attending to the words of scripture, the message of the gospel. The latter part emphasizes hearing the gospel's Lord in a time of personal and communal prayer.

Hearing and listening are for the sake of receiving and re-sponding—receiving and responding that we may be ever more transformed in the Lord's likeness and so act in union with him for the transformation of the world "so that God may be all in all" (1 Cor 15:28).

The Session Format

Gathering

As members arrive, time is quite naturally taken for people to update one another on the events of their lives since the last meeting. If some momentous event has happened in someone's life, it will receive particular attention and perhaps, some extended conversation. Ordinarily, however, this catching up time should be brief. The usual social time at the end of the session allows people additional opportunity to talk as they will. This gathering time should ordinarily take no more than ten minutes.

Opening Prayer

Conscious of time, the leader for the session calls the community to attention after the initial gathering conversation. Supported by silence, spoken prayer, music, song, or some ritual gesture, the principal focus of the opening prayer time is on inviting the members to personal and communal awareness of the presence of the God who gathers them in small community.

Hearing the Lord's Gospel

Following the opening prayer time, the scriptures from the Old Testament and the epistles are read aloud with a pause for reflection following each reading. The proclamation of the gospel follows, after which the leader invites members to name a word or phrase from the gospel text that stays with them, just a gospel word or phrase, without additional comment at this point. *(Until this pattern is well established, the leader for the session alerts the community before the proclamation of the gospel that he or she will be inviting the mention of a gospel word or phrase after the gospel's proclamation.)* Repetition of what someone else may have said is fine. What counts is that members mention the word or phrase that struck them.

When this sharing is complete, the leader poses two questions, pausing between each: What draws you to this gospel? Where do you resist this gospel? Having heard these questions, the community pauses for individual reflection. There is no immediate conversation about these questions. There will be time in the gathering of the small groups and/or in the extended conversation of the whole community that will follow the gathering in the smaller groupings.

After some time to ponder the two questions above, copies of the scriptures for the week are passed out to each member.[2] An extended time of silence is allowed for members to reflect further on the scriptures, especially the gospel, and on whatever resource material (commentary, questions) the community may be using.

Following this reflection time the leader asks members to gather in threes or fours for some conversation. These groups move apart so they do not intrude on one another. Members gather in different groupings of three or four from session to session. Some communities hesitate to break into threes or fours, saying, "We want to hear what everyone has to say." There will be time for that later in the session. At the outset, conversation in threes or fours allows for, facilitates, and encourages fuller individual participation. Gathering in the threes or fours provides the opportunity for a freer, deeper, and more ample conversation than might otherwise take place at the outset in the larger community as a whole. In exploring whatever conversation-starting questions that have been provided, members speak to whatever question(s) engage them in any particular order.

After about fifteen or twenty minutes in the small groups, the leader invites members to come together for conversation in the community as a whole. Beginning with a pause to let people collect their thoughts from the initial conversation, the leader poses these questions to the community: What do you hear God saying to you or to us in hearing and sharing his word? What do you want to hold on to for yourself from this sharing? What does God ask of you or us in light of this sharing of life and faith? Members may pick up on a thought shared in the smaller group, but they speak only for themselves. They do not report back on the sharings of others. Some new thread for reflection may emerge in the conversation of the community as a whole. These latter questions

---

[2] Copies of the weekly scriptures may be easily downloaded and printed from the website of the United States Conference of Catholic Bishops.

posed by the leader are meant to help members tie the overall conversation together and begin to transition to the extended time of prayer that follows.

Hearing the Gospel's Lord

After about twenty minutes of conversation in the whole group, the community moves to an extended time of prayer. The leader or a member of the community rereads the gospel or some key part of it aloud, after which the leader invites members to a time of silent prayer. *(On weeks that have an especially long gospel, the community may opt to use the shorter version offered in the lectionary.)* The time of prayer might also be focused around part of the week's responsorial psalm.

After the rereading of the gospel, the leader introduces the extended time of silence by asking: What does Christ in his Spirit say to you now? What do you say in response? Perhaps play a short selection of instrumental music conducive to prayer. If that is the case, the time of pure silence that follows should be very substantial.

After this extended silence the leader invites members to mention in a word or two or in a brief phrase what it is they sense Christ in his Spirit saying to them personally. This is not the time to unpack a new thought on the scriptures or to resume the conversation about the Lord's gospel. It is a time of communion with the gospel's Lord. Members simply share as they will how Christ in his Spirit seems to be addressing them personally in these moments. Without comment, the rest of the community simply receives what each offers.

Closing Prayer

When the sharing from this extended time of prayer is complete, the session concludes with some words of spoken prayer by the leader or a member; a song; an appropriate ritual gesture that might be suggested in connection with the gospel of the week; or the exchange of a sign of peace.

After-Session Social

A social that features simple refreshments usually follows each SCC session. The one who is hosting the particular session is typically the one to arrange for the refreshments. When the community meets regularly in the same place, members take turns providing the refreshments. This is a time for members to relax in one another's company. The conversation is allowed to take on a life of its own, whether members share with one another what is going on in the rest of their lives or in the world or continue some part of the community's earlier conversation. Except for special occasions, the social time is usually no longer than a half hour. Members feel free to stay or depart as their time allows.

A Note on Time and the Role of the Leader

The SCC session is designed to take about an hour and a half. Time for the social is additional. Sensitive to the various schedules and needs of the members, the session proper should begin and end on time. The session leader needs to be attuned both to the dynamics of the meeting and to how God's Spirit seems to be at work in the community, as well as to managing the time. Staying with the sequence of steps suggested, ensuring the appropriate length of the times of silence, seeing to the formation of the threes and fours, and honoring the extended time for prayer can be a challenge at times. There is a certain spiritual discipline involved in following the model proposed here. In this individualistic culture of ours, persons and communities often just prefer to do their own thing. But we gather in SCC not to do our own thing, but to do the Lord's thing: above all to hear the Lord's gospel and to hear the gospel's Lord. The leader offers a great service to the community by holding the community as a whole and individual members, as needed, to the process as it is described here. By its fruits you will know it.

Finally, for a community that might embrace this model for gathering, it would serve its members and the community as a whole well to have access to this essay and to explore it together as the members begin to come together. This model will be most fruitfully implemented when members understand the spirit of the model, along with its various steps, and agree communally to enter into it together.

Timetable for the Small Christian Community Session

Time	*Session Element*
10 min.	Gathering
5 min.	Opening Prayer
10 min.	Reading of the first two scriptures with pause; reading of the gospel
1 min.	Name a word or phrase that stays with you from the gospel
3 min.	Silent reflection: What draws you to this gospel? Where do you resist this gospel?
5 min.	Copies of the gospel distributed; read any accompanying reflection and questions; silence
15 min.	Conversation in threesomes or foursomes
20 min.	Regathering as whole community; pause; conversation
	What do you hear Christ in his Spirit saying to you/us in hearing and sharing his word?
	What do you want to hold on to from this session?

	What does God ask of us in light of our sharing of life and faith?
12 min.	Extended time of prayer
	Rereading the gospel or a part of it
	Extended silence
	What does Christ in his Spirit say to you now?
	What do you say in response?
3 min.	Name in a word or phrase what you hear Christ in his Spirit say to you now?
5 min.	Closing prayer
	(Social time)

Appendix 3

The Review of Life

A Spirituality and Method of Student Christian Communities

MICHAEL DEEB, OP

The Review of Life
and the See-Judge-Act Method

For many small communities of students around the world, the methodology of the Review of Life, often described as the see, judge, act method, is at the core of their organizational structure. Inspired by the experience of the Young Christian Worker (YCW) movement and the tradition of specialized Catholic Action, these communities live the Review of Life in many different methodical approaches. This is particularly the case for groups linked to the International Young Catholic Student (IYCS) movement. Other Catholic student groups use similar methods described by different names, including action-reflection-action and the pastoral circle. At the heart of all these methodical approaches is a common spirituality.

Parts of this chapter are adapted from Michael Deeb, *Discovering God through Action and Reflection: A Spirituality of IYCS* (International Young Catholic Students, 2004). Used with permission of IYCS.

What Do We Mean by Spirituality?

The word *spirituality* can evoke a variety of meanings, which are at times even in conflict with one other. Therefore, before we can spell out the spirituality of the Review of Life, we need to clarify the sense in which we will use the word. Basically, by *spirituality* we mean "the spirit with which we do things, because we believe that it is the way that most enables us to encounter God." There are always two dimensions to defining spirituality: by defining the *form* it takes, and by defining the *content* it contains.

The *form* that one's spirituality takes is the context, structure or mediation that every person or every group has to organize or find in order to discover, encounter, and feel closer to God, or the Truth. Some find that they encounter God more profoundly through silent meditation; others through praying the Rosary; or through singing and praying or dancing in a group; or through being outside in nature; or through working among the poor; or through being part of a large gathering or rally. There are innumerable examples.

Each of these contexts or mediations constitutes a particular spirituality—a way of awakening and encountering God's Spirit that is already within each one of us, so that it nourishes our faith and the way we live. These mediations help us to discover a sense of meaning and to set our hearts on fire.

While a particular *form* may enable different people to have a similar spiritual experience (in the sense of an emotional or motivating experience), this does not necessarily inspire the same fruits (way of living). In this sense the form of the spirituality can be neutral. Therefore, in order to complete the definition of the spirituality, we have to identify the *content* that it contains. This is the message or the way of living that we believe the Holy Spirit is calling us to pass on, which depends on how we interpret the gospel. It is the criteria we adopt to evaluate whether we are living according to the true Spirit of Jesus. While many spiritualties complement one another in awakening the Holy Spirit that lies within us, there are often spiritualties that are in contradiction. Thus, some might encourage deep involvement in the world, while others might encourage escaping from the world; or some might promote community, while others might promote individualism; or God may be seen as a compassionate friend by some and as a stern, moralistic judge by others. We are continually challenged to discern whether it is indeed the Holy Spirit that our own spirituality is awakening in us or whether it is some other spirit.

The Review of Life as lived by the IYCS and other student movements in the tradition of specialized Catholic Action offers both a form (the particular points of reference, contexts or mediations) and content (the criteria for living according to the Spirit) to enable us to encounter God.

The Roots of Review of Life Spirituality: Three Truths

The roots of the spirituality of the Review of Life lie in the "three truths in the lives of all Christians" articulated in the 1920s by Joseph (later Cardinal) Cardijn (1882–1967), the founder of the YCW movement. In his work with small groups of young industrial workers Cardijn identified three truths—life, faith, and method—as fundamental dimensions to be acknowledged if Christians are serious about communicating the good news of Christ to any sector or "specialized" group of the population:

- The *truth of life* (of *reality* or of *experience*) reveals to us that life experience for most people, even while comprising many joys, is nevertheless largely a reality of struggle, suffering, oppression, injustice, conflict, greed, exclusion, and selfishness.
- The *truth of faith,* on the other hand, assures us that we are all created in God's image. Hence, as children of God, we believe that all people are called to be co-creators in building a world that God intended, a world of love, joy, freedom,

justice, peace, sharing, solidarity, and service—the reign or kingdom of God. It is a world that, in our deepest being, we all really desire. The truth of life is thus often experienced as a total contradiction of this truth of faith.

- The *truth of method* (or of *movement* or *action*), therefore, highlights the necessity of finding a method and of building a movement to remove this contradiction—to change life experience from one of suffering and injustice to one of love and justice—and hence to bring faith and life together. Following the tradition of the prophets, Jesus began this movement, the church (of which IYCS is an integral part), which needs to be continually reminded of its task to "denounce" evil and to "announce" good news. And each Christian is personally called to be an active agent in enabling this movement to succeed in its mission.

With these assumptions about the meaning (content) of the Gospel, Cardijn developed the see-judge-act method as his answer to the search for an effective method (form) of evangelization—of bringing good news to the world by reducing the contradiction between life and faith. This process, he insisted, must always start from life—to *see* a concrete experience or issue, which is always an actual and true story, and to analyze it in order to understand its context and causes. The second step is then to *judge* the problem or issue by confronting it with the experience of faith, by searching for the feelings God would have in relation to it. The third step is to make concrete plans to *act* in the light of the preceding reflection in order to address the issue.

This process, with a continual focus on reality, the gospel, and action, is, in a nutshell, what constitutes a spirituality of action, which we call the Review of Life. It is in taking each of these focuses seriously in an ongoing process of reflection and action that we believe we are most profoundly able to encounter God, discover the truth, and thereby become God's instruments in enabling the reign of God to come. Or, in other words, the Holy

Spirit is to be discovered in a deep understanding of real-life experience, through a discerning reflection on the gospel, and through our reflective action aimed at transforming that reality. Let us now look at each of these three truths in turn and identify the specific spirituality (form and content) that they reveal.

Truth of Life: A Spirituality of Seeing the Whole of Life Concretely, Critically, and Deeply

"Seeing" concrete life experience is always the starting point (the first form) of our spirituality. We believe that God's Spirit, the Spirit of Life, is revealed as we concretely identify and critically and deeply analyze our own whole life experience with the eyes and the heart of faith, trust, and openness. This means focusing on everything that (positively or negatively) affects our own lives and the lives of the people we are living and working with. One way to get a handle on the many dimensions of life that we all experience is to consider our life and the life of each person as an "onion with many layers," with each of which we have a relationship. These relationships range from being very intimate (with ourself, our family and friends, the land and its fruit, air and water) to being less personal (with our church or our school) to being very distant (with our city, country, or the world or universe at large). Yet all of these layers (relationships) are interconnected, so that freedom and harmony or the lack of either in each layer affects the others, either directly or indirectly.

Within this form of our spirituality, the content or message we identify is that God, who created all things in harmony, is at the heart of all of this. God is within us and is at the heart of each one of these layers, looking at them from the perspective of the poor, the marginalized, and those suffering, bursting for the Holy Spirit to be manifested at every level, and trying to show the interconnectedness of each level. We are relating more intimately with God the deeper we "see," and when we can feel God's anguish and joy at each layer of our existence, from the deeply personal to

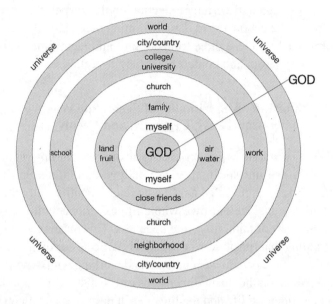

the broadly global. We are relating intimately with God when we can experience God's compassion for those who are suffering at every level. We are relating intimately with God when we allow God's Spirit to use us to bring life, freedom, and wholeness (Luke 4:18) to each layer of the humanity given to us. Thus, a central dimension of the spirituality of the Review of Life is the need to look deeply at *all* aspects (layers) of reality (the whole of life) and to seek an integration and harmony among them.

Truth of Faith: A Spirituality of Judging Reality and Our Own Values with the Eyes of Jesus Christ

Having identified and understood a real-life reality, the second form or step in the Review of Life is to take a step back and look at the issue with the eyes of faith, which, for us, are the eyes of Jesus Christ. First, we want to identify how Jesus can be made present (incarnated) in that situation, and therefore to judge how the situation corresponds to his way. Then, second, we want to identify how that situation and Jesus's response to it challenge our own values and priorities.

Thus, this moment of judging is meant to be a moment of deep conversion in the Review of Life process. Unfortunately, though, many of our groups find it very difficult to "judge"! It is normally very clear what needs to be done to "see" and to "act." We can describe an issue or problem, analyze it, and decide what we can do to respond to it or change it. Or we can describe an action, evaluate its effectiveness, and plan another action to improve the situation. However, once we have finished "seeing" the problem or the action, and reach the moment when we are supposed to "judge," we sometimes read a biblical text and briefly discuss it, or more often than not we just brush over the question and just go straight to planning an action. "Judging" is often seen as a dispensable element in the process—something it would be nice to do if we had time (which we never have, of course). This challenges us to rethink what this moment in our lives or our meetings are really for. How can the moment of "judging" enable us to encounter God more deeply?

The first point that we have to appreciate is that every decision to act presumes a conscious or unconscious judgment beforehand—about what needs to be done to make the situation better. Judging is essentially a moment to ensure that our decisions are not based on the unconscious assumptions that we have always had, but rather on a thorough, deep, and critical reflection and evaluation of the reality, issue, or problem that we have identified.

In order to make a judgment, we always need to choose criteria. As Christians, our chief criterion is the person of Jesus (his life, words, actions, and spirit), the knowledge of whom our tradition, stemming from the apostles, has passed on to us through scripture. The Bible, especially the Gospels, offers us an indispensable lens to judge. Knowledge of and active engagement with Jesus Christ in the scriptures is clearly essential for leaders of small groups.

But it is not enough just to look at scripture, for various reasons. First, there are many different interpretations of the same text even among learned theologians. Second, the gospel does not have something direct to say on every situation and context with which we are faced, since the world has changed enormously, and many new issues and situations have arisen that the people of Jesus's time could not even have contemplated. Third, we can be tempted to seek biblical texts that use the same words as us in order to justify whatever judgment or action we have already decided is appropriate—which would add nothing new to our judgment. Or we can be tempted to apply a text directly to our situation without taking into account its meaning in its particular context or time, which may be vastly different from our own.

In the light of this reality the church, through the ages, in the teachings of its pastors and in the works of theologians, has continually sought to identify anew Jesus's spirit (the Holy Spirit) in the major issues facing people in their lives. This has resulted in a rich reservoir of authoritative texts from church councils, popes, and bishops, including Catholic social teachings, which show how the church is constantly evolving in its appreciation of the gospel truth and therefore always renewing itself. Small groups therefore need to refer to and use this evolving tradition as a vital lens (criterion) for judging situations.

Over the past fifty years student groups within IYCS and IMCS, undertaking this deeper analysis, have repeatedly reaffirmed the content of their spirituality. Drawing from scripture, Catholic doctrine, contextual theologies, and the experiences of students worldwide, we affirm our belief that Jesus revealed to us a God who is present in the world and whose priority is to bring about a kingdom or reign in continuity with this world (Mark 1:15; Luke 17:21; Matt 12:28; 25:31–46). In this reign all people, especially the poor and marginalized, are freed (saved) from all forms of oppression (Luke 4:18; 6:20–25) and dependency (John 5:1–9), and each has equal dignity (Matt 23:1–12); it is a world of love and justice, with a spirit of sharing (Matt 19:16–22) and service (Mark 10:41–45) that enables unity, solidarity and harmony to exist for everyone. This faith motivates us to promote such a new world—in other words, to evangelize.

We can thus assert that the above theology—which is rooted in critical reflection and action for a better world, that is, the reign of God—corresponds most closely to the truth of our faith reflection and experience so far. It therefore defines our criteria for making our judgments of reality and of our own values with the eyes of Jesus Christ. It constitutes the content of our spirituality, which can be captured in the following prayer:

> Loving God,
> Thank you for the many gifts you have given to me,
> Even though I have done nothing to deserve them.
> Give me the wisdom to see myself, to see others, and
>   to see the world with your eyes,
> the eyes of Jesus, your Son.
> In all my encounters, give me the compassion to feel
>   what those on all sides are feeling,
> especially those who are poor or suffering.
> Give me the strength and courage of the Holy Spirit to
>   change what is not in your plan
> of love, justice, mercy and peace.
> And give me the faith to know that all my successes
>   and failures come from you,
> and that they bring neither glory nor shame to me.
>
>   Amen.

Truth of Method: A Spirituality of Action Aimed at Transforming Our Life Experience

Having judged a life reality with the eyes of faith, and having identified any contradiction that might exist between that reality and Jesus's vision of God's reign, we are then faced with the task of identifying a way (a method) and an action that will remove that contradiction. This will reinforce the growth of the movement that is seeking to integrate life and faith. It is in the process of engaging in such Spirit-filled action—the final form of the Review of Life spirituality, which is a spirituality of action—that we believe we encounter and come to know God most profoundly (Jas 2:14–26).

The Review of Life is geared toward *action*. Why is this? Because we want to make a difference to our world. We want to change it. And we cannot do this only by talking or praying (even though these are also indispensable). We have to *do* things that will make that difference. In every group or organization people do many things, but in the context of the Review of Life, an action is not just any action.

An action is something we do which *emerges out of our reflection on a concrete experience* that we have actually encountered, so that everyone "owns" it and feels passionately about implementing it. Hence it is not simply a habitual activity organized only by the leaders of a group. It is something planned by all the members—preferably in a small group. And it has the aim of transforming the life experience encountered by the students—something that will make a difference. Of course, many activities can also be actions, but only if they emerge as a response to an experience that needs to be addressed, with the aim of transforming it (such as the realization of a need for a particular formation for individuals or the group). And to be spiritually nourishing, an action must also be followed by reflection, so that we can appreciate why we are doing it, and what effect it has had on us and on the world. If this is missing, we can easily lose the sense of the action and descend into simple activism, which can then easily become misdirected.

Also, for us, an action is not necessarily something big involving a lot of people (like a big conference, or a rally). It can be just an attempt to talk to someone about the issue in question. The basic principle is that no action is too small. The parable of the mustard seed (Mark 4:30–32) is a good example of the meaning of action in our movement.

The smallest of seeds can end up being the biggest shrub of them all. Even the smallest action can end up having an effect way beyond what we can imagine. And it is in doing something, even something very small, to address a problem identified that we find hope. If we are conscious that what we are doing is an action, it helps us to believe that we can make a difference, and therefore that things can change. It also helps us to overcome a mentality of dependency, in which we see salvation as something that only comes from outside.

Thus, reflective and conscious engagement in action enables us to encounter God more deeply in the discovery of hope, in making a positive difference in people's lives, and in building communities and small groups that seek to make God's kingdom of freedom, justice, and peace present in our world.

Conclusion

The spirituality of Review of Life is thus a process with a continual focus on reality, the gospel, and action. It is in taking each of these focuses seriously in an ongoing process of deepening our understanding of real-life experience, of discerning reflection on the gospel, and of reflective action aimed at transforming our reality that we believe we are most profoundly able to encounter God, discover the truth, and thereby become God's instruments in enabling the reign of God to come.

Implicit in each of these focuses are certain convictions about the meaning (content) of the gospel, and of the methods (form) of evangelization necessary to reduce the contradiction between life and faith. The methodology of see-judge-act is an important way to live this spirituality, but there are risks that the methodology can become mechanistic, rigid, boring, and even oppressive—precisely the opposite of the world we are trying to build.

Thus, while it is extremely valuable (and maybe even necessary) to use this method (form) to arrive at our goal, it is important to avoid seeing it in narrow terms. It is less a rigid, mechanistic formula than a reminder for us continually to keep in broad view the three dimensions of *focus on reality*, *focus on faith*, and *focus on transforming action*. This will enable us to maintain a priority focus on the content of our spirituality—the criteria we use for evaluating our practice—without getting bogged down in language about methodology. It will also enable us to consciously benefit from the variety of other methodologies that we tend to use anyway (biblical studies, immersion programs, service projects, silent meditation, and so on), and that can help us to deepen our grasp of each of these three dimensions.

Thus, through the Review of Life, we are trying to empower students to gain a deeper awareness of God in their lives, their schools, our church, and our world by giving them the space (preferably in small groups) to reflect deeply on their personal experience, to evaluate it, and then to act to transform each of these domains. When we develop this capacity, we will truly become a movement that is building leaders who are full of hope and who will have a major impact in inspiring the faith that will enable God's kingdom to become a reality in our world.

Appendix 4

Outline for Using the Review of Life (See-Judge-Act) Method in Small Groups

KEVIN AHERN

The following is a sample outline for a Review of Life group. Ideally, the method is best lived in a community of five to ten students that meets weekly. The see-judge-act method presented here should not be understood in a rigid way. Each small group should adapt this method to its different realities and contexts. After living this method a few times, the rhythm of the Review of Life will gradually become clear.

Review of Life at a Glance

10 min.	Opening Prayer and Gospel Reading
5 min.	Brief Review of Past Actions
15 min.	See: Sharing the Experience of Life / What is happening and why?
15 min.	Judge: Theological Analysis / What does this mean in light of scripture and the Catholic tradition?

| 15 min. | Act: Witnessing to God's Kingdom / How are we called to respond? |
| 5 min. | Closing Prayer / prayers of petition, Lord's Prayer, Sign of Peace |

Gathering a Small Community

The method works best if participants can come to the meetings in a spirit of openness and trust. Many groups who use the Review of Life, for example, organize a shared meal or social outing following the meeting. Some go together on trips to religious sites or to witness the work of an organization working for social change. We cannot expect students to open up to one another if they do not know one another, and this takes effort. Close friendships and romantic relationships often develop within communities, and these should be celebrated. Attention, however, must be paid to ensure close friendships do not exclude anyone or disrupt the overall dynamics of the community.

Group Leadership and Dynamics

Each meeting should have an animator to lead the specific meeting and to be watchful of the time. Student animators or leaders may be selected by their peers to lead one meeting or for a set time period. A young professional, campus minister, or chaplain may serve as the animator of the group at the early stages, but the goal should be to enable each member to serve as a leader in some capacity. Distributing roles throughout the meeting (prayers, readers, food preparers, and so forth) can help to create a participatory atmosphere. The group may also discern or elect a team of students to organize the meetings and represent them with larger groups. As the community grows, new members may join and some experienced leaders may even be commissioned to start or animate a new group.

Before the Meeting

Participants should come to the meeting prepared: remembering the community in one's personal prayer life, being ready to share an experience with the group, and recalling the discussions from the last meeting.

Opening the Meeting with the Gospel

After any brief announcements, the meeting should begin with prayer and scripture. The opening prayer, ideally, should include a reading from scripture. The Gospel reading of that week is advisable as it connects the group with the whole church.

Reviewing Past Actions

Before taking up a new experience, the community should review commitments decided from the last gathering by asking, for example: Have we followed up on the commitments we made? If yes, what results did we see? If no, why not?

This need not take a lot of time. And if the action needs more thought and reflection, the group may decide to focus on this for the rest of the meeting. Otherwise, the community should move to address new experiences using the see-judge-act method.

See: Sharing the Experience of Life

The first stage in the Review of Life process is sharing experience. Each Christian, no matter what age or socioeconomic status, experiences contradictions between the Christian faith and daily life. What does this look like for students today?

Sharing experiences: Each member of the group is invited to briefly share a "fact" or recent experience with the group. These should be personal and concrete experiences of joys, hopes, sorrows, and anxieties. For example, a student may share an experience of racial discrimination in the university, a joy in witnessing an act of charity by a fellow student, or a concern about recycling on campus.

Selecting one experience to examine: After the brief sharing, the community selects one urgent and challenging experience to "see with the eyes of Christ." The participant who shared the experience is then invited to explain in more detail what happened and who was involved.

Seeing more clearly: Other members of the group can now share in this experience by asking questions such as:

- Have you witnessed a similar situation or do you have similar concerns? If yes, explain?
- Is this an isolated incident or a symptom of a deeper issue?
- What do you see as some of the deeper causes, including structural, economic, social, and environmental, that encourage or support such experiences? (Do not spend too much time in what Pope Francis describes as "excessive diagnosis.")
- Who benefits? Who suffers? Why?

Judge: Theological Analysis

The second stage of the Review of Life opens the door to thinking more critically and deeply in a discerning way. This theological analysis works best if we see it as a moment of prayer, a reflection with God, with openness to conversion. Here, we are invited to examine the experience selected by the community with a gospel lens:

- What virtues or values do we see? What prejudices, vices or sins can we identify?
- How are we implicated in this experience? Have we committed acts of commission or omission that might support such a situation and/or the underlying social structures? Have we

been indifferent? How does this experience relate to the teachings of Jesus Christ and the kingdom of God that he preached?

- How does the tradition of the church (the lives of saints, Catholic social teaching, and so on) inform this experience?
- What can be done at a personal and collective level to address this situation?

Act: Witnessing to God's Kingdom

The third stage opens up a space for personal and collective transformation. Here, the group is invited to identify concrete actions that can be taken to address the experience in light of Christian faith. These actions should be both practical and prophetic. In other words, they should be able to be accomplished but also be challenging and transformative. For example, "we will end homelessness" is not an achievable goal, but finding a room for a specific family in a local parish or setting up a meeting with the city council to discuss housing policy could be.

- What are we being called to do? As persons? As a group?
- Who is going to do what, when, where, and how?
- In light of this experience, what do we need to change in ourselves and our relationships with others to better embody the values of God's Kingdom?
- How will we evaluate our action at the next meeting?

Closing Prayer

As the group winds down, it is time to end the meeting with prayer. These prayers should be done in a spirit of thanksgiving for God's presence in the meeting and in our lives. Many groups conclude with open prayers of petition for members to bring their hopes and sorrows before God, followed by a recitation of the Lord's Prayer and a sign of peace.

Appendix 5

A Brief Guide
for Communal Discernment

KEVIN AHERN

> *Ministry in a missionary key seeks to aban-*
> *don the complacent attitude that says: "We*
> *have always done it this way." I invite ev-*
> *eryone to be bold and creative in this task*
> *of rethinking the goals, structures, style*
> *and methods of evangelization in their re-*
> *spective communities. A proposal of goals*
> *without an adequate communal search for*
> *the means of achieving them will inevitably*
> *prove illusory.*
> —POPE FRANCIS, *EVANGELII GAUDIUM*, NO. 33

In the above quotation Pope Francis reminds us of the need for church structures, including small communities of students, to adopt a discerning spirit and to reflect on what we are doing, why we are doing it, and how we are getting it done. In other words, church communities must find ways to reflect prayerfully on their identity, mission, and organization. To this end it is important for student communities and campus ministry programs to take time every so often, perhaps every year or two, for a moment of communal discernment: this may include a general checkup, a mission assessment, and/or exercises in communal self-care.

This process should involve all the members of the community. Friendly outsiders from other communities or campuses could be invited to help facilitate a conversation if that is deemed beneficial.

The following questions[1] offer a basis for a communal discernment and assessment process:

Who are we as a student community (identity)?

- Who are we? Do we have a mission or identity statement?
- How do we embody the six dimensions of campus ministry?[2]
- How do we see God or grace (Holy Spirit) acting within our community?
- How do we relate to the local church (parishes, diocese)?
- How do we relate to the poor and the marginalized?
- Are we part of any national or global network of similar groups?
- What are the biggest strengths and weaknesses of our community?
- What have been our successes and failures over the past year?
- Are there any community members who feel marginalized?
- Have people left or joined recently? If yes, why?
- What resources, including human and financial, do we have?

---

[1] These questions are adapted from Kevin Ahern, *Structures of Grace: Catholic Organizations Serving the Global Common Good* (Maryknoll, NY: Orbis Books, 2015).

[2] These six, as identified by the US Catholic Bishops in *Empowered by the Spirit,* are forming the faith community, appropriating the faith; forming Christian conscience, educating for peace and justice, facilitating personal development, and developing leaders for the future.

Where is God calling our community to go (mission)?

- What are the hopes and needs of our members?
- What are the needs of the church?
- How do we relate to the poor and the marginalized?
- Where might we imagine Jesus Christ calling us to go?
- What are the current needs of the wider community (college community, city, nation, world)?
- How does the Gospel challenge our community?

What do we need to do to get there (organization)?

- What actions, tactics, or structures are necessary to better serve our mission?
- Who are potential allies for our mission?
- What resources (including human, financial, and logistical) are needed?
- Who will do what and by when?
- What arrangements are needed to ensure participation and accountability in the life of the movement?
- How will we evaluate our progress?

Appendix 6

Resource Organizations

The Catholic Campus Ministry Association (CCMA) is the professional association for Catholic campus ministers across the United States. Providing annual, quarterly, and monthly resources for campus ministers, in person and online, CCMA equips Catholic campus ministers to carry out the new evangelization. www.ccmanet.org.

Catholic Relief Services' University Engagement invites Catholic colleges and universities, as well as Catholic organizations on other campuses, to join us in solidarity with the global poor through education, prayer, and action. The CRS Student Ambassador program engages college students in tangible acts of solidarity to build a more just and peaceful world. Colleges and universities form on-campus chapters of student leaders who are trained by CRS to mobilize their peers and bring to life the mission of global solidarity. Chapters are connected to one another and to CRS in order to build a national movement for effective change. www.university.crs.org.

The Christian Life Community (CLC) is an international association of Christians, men and women, adults and young people, of all social conditions, who want to follow Jesus Christ more closely and work with him for the building of the kingdom. Members make up small groups, which are part of larger communities organized regionally and nationally, all forming one world community. The CLC is present in all five continents, in more than sixty countries. The charism and spirituality of CLC are Ignatian. Thus, the *Spiritual Exercises* of St. Ignatius are both the specific source of CLC charism and the characteristic instrument of CLC spirituality. The CLC way of life is shaped by the features of Ignatian Christology: austere and simple, in solidarity with the poor and the outcasts of society, integrating contemplation and action, in all things living lives of love and service within the church, always in a spirit of discernment. www.cvx-clc.net.

Small Christian Communities (SCCs) Global Collaborative Website envisions establishing a global networking website for SCCs worldwide. It shares SCCs contact information, events, materials, and news for Africa, Asia, Europe, Latin America, North America, and Oceania. www.smallchristiancommunities.org.

Engaging Students to Enliven the Ecclesial Mission (ESTEEM) is a nationwide program to develop the leadership skills of young Catholic students at private, Catholic, and secular colleges and universities across the nation. It is a project of the National Leadership Roundtable on Church Management in collaboration with Saint Thomas More Catholic Chapel and Center at Yale University. www.esteemleadership.org.

The Evangelical Catholic equips Catholic ministries for evangelization by inspiring, training, and supporting local leaders to drive dynamic outreach. www.evangelicalcatholic.org

The Fellowship of Catholic University Students (FOCUS) is a Catholic collegiate outreach whose mission is to share the hope and joy of the gospel with college and university students. Trained in church teaching, prayer, scripture, evangelization, and discipleship, FOCUS missionaries encounter students in friendship where they are, inviting them into a personal relationship with Jesus Christ and accompanying them as they pursue lives of virtue and excellence. Through Bible studies, outreach events, mission trips, and one-on-one discipleship, missionaries inspire and build up students in the faith, sending them out to spread the good news and to live out the Great Commission: "Go, therefore, and make disciples of all nations" (Matt 28:19). www.focus.org.

The International Catholic Movement for Intellectual and Cultural Affairs (ICMICA–Pax Romana) is a global community of Catholic professionals engaged in the world with a spirituality of action. Inspired by the gospel and the Catholic social tradition, ICMICA seeks to live faith by engaging the challenges of our times. As a movement, ICMICA is committed to the option for the poor, integral human development, and the empowerment of women and young professionals. ICMICA brings together professionals, often in small groups, to support one another and to offer a voice in international forums, including the Vatican and the United Nations system. www.icmica-miic.org.

The International Movement of Catholic Students–Pax Romana (IMCS) is a global movement of Catholic university students and student movements. IMCS was founded by students in 1921 with the name Pax Romana to express their desire to build peace and solidarity in a world torn apart by war. Since then, IMCS has grown to include over eighty diverse national movements of Catholic university students and student movements, many with their own distinctive names and ways of evangelizing. IMCS is recognized as an international association of the faithful by the Holy See and as a nongovernmental organization in consultative status with the United Nations Economic and Social Council. www.imcs-miec.org.

The International Young Catholic Students (IYCS) is a movement of specialized Catholic Action. It is an evangelization agent in schools and student milieu (secondary and higher education). IYCS is present in eighty-seven countries. Inspired by the spirituality of Cardinal Joseph Cardijn (the founder of the Young Christian Workers), IYCS has a spirituality of reflection and action that helps young people to the internalization of faith and to match their life to the gospel. It is through the methodology of the Review of Life (see-judge-act) that IYCS provides formation and raises youth engagement in their realities. It is engagement that translates in mobilization and action against poverty, exclusion and injustice in the world, and a commitment to be in service of the poorest of the poor. www.iycs-jeci.org.

RENEW International fosters spiritual renewal in the Catholic tradition by empowering individuals and communities to encounter God in everyday life, deepen and share faith, and connect faith with action. Campus RENEW is a two-and-a-half-year (or five semester) process that facilitates renewal and transformation on college campuses. Small Christian communities, groups of eight to twelve students who come together weekly to share faith, are the building blocks of this process. These communities create opportunities for students to experience community and spirituality and to be challenged outward to service. www.renewintl.org.

St. Paul's Outreach actively invites college students to a life of Christian discipleship. With St. Paul as our example, we create vibrant, faith-filled environments that challenge students to deepen their relationships with Christ in the fullness of the Catholic Church. Our core values include renewed Catholicism, missionary dedication to the new evangelization, life-changing communities, servant leadership, and Christian unity. www.spo.org.

USCCB Committee on Catholic Education provides guidance for the educational mission of the church in the United States in all its institutional settings. It guides, directs, and coordinates this task, working closely with the Committee on Evangelization and Catechesis. The scope of the Committee on Catholic Education's work includes Catholic elementary and secondary schools, Catholic colleges and universities, and college campus ministry. The committee advocates for federal public policies in education that are consistent with Catholic values and that uphold parental rights and responsibilities regarding education. www.usccb.org.

Contributors

Kevin Ahern, a husband and father, is an assistant professor of religious studies at Manhattan College, where he directs the Peace Studies program. He is the past president of the IMCS (2003–7) and the author of *Structures of Grace: Catholic Organizations Serving the Global Common Good* (Orbis Books). @kevin_ahern

Robert Beloin, a priest of the Archdiocese of Hartford, was ordained in 1973. He has served in parish ministries as an assistant pastor and pastor, and in seminary formation as director of pastoral formation at the American College in Louvain. He has been the chaplain at St. Thomas More Chapel and Center at Yale University since 1994. @STMatYale

Afou Chantal Bengaly, a wife and mother, holds a doctorate in pharmacy from the University of Bamako–Mali and a master's degree in international health from Jomo Kenyatta University of Agriculture and Technology Kenya. She is former Pan African Program Coordinator of the IMCS (2011–15), former chairperson for the Network of International Youth Organization in Africa (2012–15). She is currently working as program manager at Wetlands International Mali and is the founder of the Association pour le Developpement Intégrale des Jeunes.

Christine Cichello is a campus minister at Boston College and works primarily with the CLC (Christian Life Community) program. She is the New England representative on the National

Coordinating Council of CLC-USA. She has master's degrees in theological studies and Lonergan Studies, as well as undergraduate degrees in math and philosophy, all from Boston College.

Marina D'Costa is a trained anthropologist. She is currently working as a researcher in the field of tobacco cessation for an organization based in Mumbai (India). She is the founder of "The Power of Dialogue" banner. She is the former co-convener for AICUF, IMCS-India.

Michael Deeb, OP, a native of South Africa, is the permanent delegate of the Dominican Order to the United Nations and the order's general promoter for justice and peace. Fr. Deeb served as the international chaplain of IMCS and IYCS from 1999 to 2007. @Doms_at_UN

Cecilia Flores is a wife, mother, and former international missionary who now serves as the director of the Newman Catholic Center of Sacramento, California. She holds a master of arts degree in global development and social justice from St. John's University, New York.

Lois Harr holds an MA in religious studies from St. Joseph's Seminary and a professional diploma in religious education from Fordham University, and she has participated in and facilitated a number of Lasallian formation programs. She is an assistant vice president in student life, serving as director of campus ministry and social action at Manhattan College. She also teaches an experiential learning course in Catholic social thought.

Joseph Healey, MM, is an American Maryknoll missionary priest who lives in Nairobi, Kenya. He came to Kenya in 1968. He teaches "Small Christian Communities (SCCs) as a New Model of Church in Africa Today" at Tangaza University College in Nairobi and a similar course at Hekima University College in Nairobi. He co-authored *Small Christian Communities Today: Capturing the New Moment* (Orbis Books and Paulines Publications Africa) and is the moderator of the Small Christian Communities (SCCs) Global Collaborative Website, www.smallchristiancommunities. org. JGHealey@aol.com

Edouard Karoue serves as the president of the International Movement of Catholic Students. A native of Togo, Edouard was elected to serve on the IMCS International Team for four years and is presently based in Paris, where he is completing his mission in service to students worldwide.

Kim Lamberty, is director of university engagement at Catholic Relief Services. Dr. Lamberty is an expert on the intersection of Catholic mission and Catholic social teaching, and she is the author of numerous articles and a book on mission and international development. She is also a founder of Just Haiti, a coffee development program based on the principles of Catholic social teaching. She holds a DMin from Catholic Theological Union, an MA from Washington Theological Union, and an MIA (master's in international affairs) from Columbia University.

Christopher Derige Malano has served in university ministry at the local, national, and international levels for two decades as a student leader and professional. Christopher is a past secretary general of the IMCS and currently serves as the pastoral administrator of the Newman Center at the University of Hawai'i–Mānoa. @cdmalano

Evelina Manola is the secretary general of the International Movement of Catholic Students. She grew up in Syros, a small island in Greece, and studied social work in Athens. She worked for Caritas Hellas before her election to the IMCS International Team.

Michael T. Martin, OFM Conv, has served as the director of the Duke Catholic Center since 2010. Previously he served as president of his high school alma mater, Archbishop Curley High School in Baltimore, Maryland. He holds an STB degree in theology from the Pontifical Theological Faculty at St. Bonaventure–The Seraphicum in Rome, Italy, an MEd in Catholic education administration from Boston College, and a bachelor's degree in philosophy from St. Hyacinth College–Seminary in Granby, Massachusetts. He has served on a number of boards and commissions and is a highlighted presenter on strategic issues facing Catholic schools today and the important role of advancement in sustaining the mission of Catholic education and campus ministry. In 2007 he received the Pro Eccelsia et Pontifice medal for service to the Church from Pope Benedict XVI. @TheDukePriest

Robert Moriarty, SM, a member of the Society of Mary (Marianists), served as director of the Pastoral Department for Small Christian Communities (Archdiocese of Hartford) from 1989 to 2017.

Nancy Njehia is a member of the Interim Eastern Africa Small Christian Community Training Team and Re-Igniters of Youth Small Christian Communities. She earned her undergraduate degree in community resource management at Kenyatta University, Nairobi, Kenya. nancynjehia2@gmail.com

Evelyn Nyaituga is a YSCC coordinator in Dandora Parish, Nairobi, Kenya. everlnenyaituga@gmail.com

Alloys Nyakundi is a member of the Eastern Africa Small Christian Community Training Team and founder of Re-Igniters of Youth Small Christian Communities. He earned his undergraduate degree in education arts at Kenyatta University, Nairobi, Kenya, and is currently completing his master's degree in pastoral studies focusing on SCCs at the University, New Orleans, Louisiana. alloysnyakundi8@gmail.com

Brian Omondi is a YSCC coordinator in Dandora Parish, Nairobi, Kenya. He is also a human rights activist and social justice champion. brianjamesomondi@gmail.com

Danielle Roberts currently works on the university engagement team at Catholic Relief Services, where she oversees the CRS Student Ambassador program. Prior to working at CRS, Danielle spent a year with the postgraduate volunteer program Rostro de Cristo in Ecuador and then worked in the program's US office for an additional year, coordinating immersion groups, recruitment, and volunteer formation. She holds a master's degree in theology from Boston College's School of Theology and Ministry and a bachelor's degree in religious studies from the University of Toledo.

Jennifer Robinson is a dual graduate of Manhattan College with a bachelor's degree in psychology and a master's degree in counseling. She started working in campus ministry and social action at Manhattan College in 2008 as a coordinator for social action and was promoted to assistant director in 2015. Jennifer coordinates the college's service immersion trips program, called Lasallian Outreach Volunteer Experience, or LOVE.

Abigail Ruskey was raised in an agnostic family in Peoria, Illinois, where she first discovered the Catholic faith as a young girl through St. Charbel Parish. She attended Purdue University in Lafayette, Indiana, receiving a bachelor of arts in linguistics, German, and Italian in 2016. She converted to Catholicism as a freshman in 2013 and is now serving in her second year as a FOCUS missionary at the University of Wisconsin–La Crosse.

Michael St. Pierre is the executive director of the Catholic Campus Ministry Association. As an author, speaker, and leader, Dr. St. Pierre supports campus ministers on over 350 campuses across the United States. Married for over twenty years, Dr.

St. Pierre and his wife, Cary, are the parents of four children. They reside in northern New Jersey. On Twitter: @mikekstpierre

Luigi Santoro is FUCI national vice president and studies law at Università degli Studi Mediterranea in Reggio Calabria, Italy.

Gabriella Serra is FUCI national president and studies law at Università Cattolica del Sacro Cuore in Milan, Italy.

Cecilia Tovar S., mother of three children and also a grandmother, has earned doctorates from the Pontifical Catholic University of Peru and the Catholic University of Leuven, Belgium. She was a member of the National Union of Catholic Students from 1964 to 1967, and she has been a member of the Movement of Catholic Professionals of Peru since its creation in 1983. She is the co-founder of the Bartolomé de Las Casas Institute, where she works.